# Setting Up Your Sewing Space

## From Small Areas to Complete Workshops

◆

## Myrna Giesbrecht

 STERLING PUBLISHING CO., INC.  NEW YORK

Dedicated to:

The creator of dreams who allowed the blinking cursor to turn
into a manuscript, the manuscript into a book and the dream into
a reality. Thank you, Lord.

My constant companion, Kyle Howard Giesbrecht, whose in-utero
critique accompanied the development of this manuscript and
who arrived on September 25, 1993. Mommy loves you.

My mother, Lynn Hodges, whose flair and skill for organization
makes me look like a total slob, but who somehow managed to
teach me to pick it up and put it away. I hear echoes of her voice
in mine. And, my father, Ken Hodges, who taught me to be
optimistic, to persevere, to keep trying even when things get
tough, and to accomplish. Thank you both.

**Library of Congress Cataloging-in-Publication Data**

Giesbrecht, Myrna.
     Setting up your sewing space : from small areas to complete
workshops / Myrna Giesbrecht.
          p.     cm.
     Includes index.
     ISBN 0-8069-0495-X
     1. Sewing—Equipment and supplies.   2. Sewing.   3. Workshops—
Design and construction.   I. Title.
TT715.G53     1994
646.2—dc20                                               93-43910
                                                              CIP

Photography for color insert by Sharon Cade.

Edited by Isabel Stein

10   9   8   7   6   5   4   3   2

Published by Sterling Publishing Company, Inc.
387 Park Avenue South, New York, N.Y. 10016
© 1994 by Myrna Giesbrecht
Distributed in Canada by Sterling Publishing
% Canadian Manda Group, P.O. Box 920, Station U
Toronto, Ontario, Canada M8Z 5P9
Distributed in Great Britain and Europe by Cassell PLC
Villiers House, 41/47 Strand, London WC2N 5JE, England
Distributed in Australia by Capricorn Link (Australia) Pty Ltd.
P.O. Box 6651, Baulkham Hills, Business Centre, NSW 2153, Australia
*Manufactured in the United States of America*
*All rights reserved*

Sterling ISBN 0-8069-0495-X

# Contents

[Color illustrations of rooms are after page 128]

# Preface

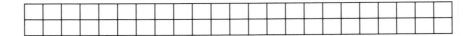

"A place for everything and everything in its place." How many of us have heard that expression more than a couple of times? Ever passed it off as some frantic housekeeper's justification for spending the entire day elbow-deep in cleaning solutions?

My philosophy had always been that as long as I knew where something was it didn't really matter if anyone else could find it. That was until I became hopelessly addicted to sewing. Pretty soon I was surrounded by piles of fabric, pattern pieces, and instructions. You name it, it was there. But, I couldn't find anything! Where are the scissors? Has anyone seen my interfacing? What about pattern piece #11? What is pattern piece #11? Has anyone seen the instructions? What am I sewing with this fabric? Where is the pattern envelope?

Does any of this sound familiar to you? Have you ever made a New Year's resolution to complete all those unfinished projects and then spent the entire month of January sewing summer fashions in fabrics and styles you didn't even like anymore? I have, and that's when I decided to get organized, to get my act in gear and "shape up" so I could "sew out" more efficiently with less frustration and a lot more fun.

Now before you get the mistaken idea that all of this occurred overnight and that I'm a super organized, lean, mean sewing machine, let me tell you that there are still days when I can't find pattern piece #11. I will be the first to say that I own six (yes six!) measuring tapes. That one elusive item refuses to be organized. However, after carefully analyzing the who, what, when, where, why, and how of my sewing room, I was able to design an environment in which I can now function more efficiently and creatively. It's my hope that you will be able to use these ideas to create an environment of your own, regardless of its size, in which you can exercise your greatest creative abilities and "sew until you drop."

# Acknowledgments

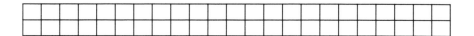

When I started this project it seemed like such an easy thing to do. Buy a computer, write a book, get published, and become an author. Wrong! Without the help of a lot of people, it would have been impossible to accomplish this dream. Consequently, I need to thank the following:

- My husband, Howard Giesbrecht, who dealt with deadlines and a highly stressed wife with constant support and encouragement. Thanks for holding my hand.
- Dave Burkholder and Ben Giudici for saving me from many a computer crisis. It's finally all on disk.
- Paul Seal for his willingness to help with Autocad and 3D Studio and to answer my myriad questions. Wish things had worked out differently.
- Ruth Swindon, for reading and rereading the text without rewriting it!
- Rhonda Lamarche, illustrator. Special thanks for the long hours and extra effort. Not only do I appreciate your skills and talents but your enthusiasm, support, and sense of professionalism.
- Sharon Cade, photographer extraordinaire. Through rain, snow, sleet, or blizzard the shoot must go on!
- Gord Wiens for electrical know-how.

# Metric Equivalents Table

| Inches | MM | CM | Inches | CM | Inches | CM |
|--------|----|----|--------|----|--------|----|
| ⅛ | 3 | 0.3 | 9 | 22.9 | 30 | 76.2 |
| ¼ | 6 | 0.6 | 10 | 25.4 | 31 | 78.7 |
| ⅜ | 10 | 1.0 | 11 | 27.9 | 32 | 81.3 |
| ½ | 13 | 1.3 | 12 | 30.5 | 33 | 83.8 |
| ⅝ | 16 | 1.6 | 13 | 33.0 | 34 | 86.4 |
| ¾ | 19 | 1.9 | 14 | 35.6 | 35 | 88.9 |
| ⅞ | 22 | 2.2 | 15 | 38.1 | 36 | 91.4 |
| 1 | 25 | 2.5 | 16 | 40.6 | 37 | 94.0 |
| 1¼ | 32 | 3.2 | 17 | 43.2 | 38 | 96.5 |
| 1½ | 38 | 3.8 | 18 | 45.7 | 39 | 99.1 |
| 1¾ | 44 | 4.4 | 19 | 48.3 | 40 | 101.6 |
| 2 | 51 | 5.1 | 20 | 50.8 | 41 | 104.1 |
| 2½ | 64 | 6.4 | 21 | 53.3 | 42 | 106.7 |
| 3 | 76 | 7.6 | 22 | 55.9 | 43 | 109.2 |
| 3½ | 89 | 8.9 | 23 | 58.4 | 44 | 111.8 |
| 4 | 102 | 10.2 | 24 | 61.0 | 45 | 114.3 |
| 4½ | 114 | 11.4 | 25 | 63.5 | 46 | 116.8 |
| 5 | 127 | 12.7 | 26 | 66.0 | 47 | 119.4 |
| 6 | 152 | 15.2 | 27 | 68.6 | 48 | 121.9 |
| 7 | 178 | 17.8 | 28 | 71.1 | 49 | 124.5 |
| 8 | 203 | 20.3 | 29 | 73.7 | 50 | 127.0 |

*MM—millimetres*    *CM—centimetres*

# PART ONE

# Organizing Space

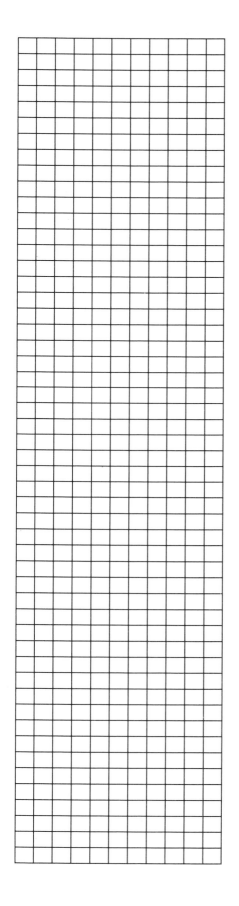

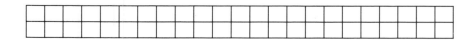

## · 1 ·

# The Five W Approach to Organization

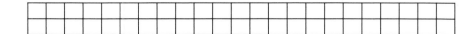

In order to design your sewing space to operate efficiently, you need to analyze exactly what's going to occur there and who's going to accomplish what. Use the following descriptions and the accompanying Personal Profile (p. 14) to prioritize specific, immediate, and long-term needs.

## WHO WILL WORK THERE?

Prior to the room-planning stage, begin by defining who will be working in the area. Unless you know this, the space cannot operate with maximum efficiency. It's impossible for two people to function in an area designed for one—sort of like too many cooks in the kitchen. Instead of feeling creative, you'll become frustrated from constantly bumping into each other or waiting for tools the other person is using.

My present sewing room is completely different from the one I designed in our previous home. As my daughter is now learning to sew, the room was planned to accommodate both of us. Also, I frequently invite friends over to sew with me, therefore I need space to set up their equipment. It's probably obvious I now have a fairly large sewing room. In fact, the longer it took to get that area of the house completed, the bigger it became.

While it's possible to design a functional sewing space in as small an area as a 5′ × 5′ closet, it would be unreasonable to expect two people to function in an area that size. Be realistic about the amount of space being set aside. Make sure it will be sufficient to meet the demands placed on it.

## WHAT WILL BE DONE THERE?

Sixteen years ago when I sewed my first seam, I didn't realize that I had just made one of the most significant discoveries of my life. Today I sew clothes for myself and my family. I make quilts, pillows, place mats, table rounds, bed skirts, fabric lampshades, curtains, valances, stuffed toys, Christmas decorations, and just about anything else that can be created out of fabric. Basically, I'm a fabriholic and, much to the disgust of some of my nonsewing friends, I find it relaxing to be in the sewing room surrounded by mounds of visual and tactile textures. I live, eat, and breathe fabric. Consequently, the space I work in has to meet many demands.

When I began designing my space, I reached for the stars and wrote down every possible function I hoped to accomplish in that area. Within one space, I wanted to cut out patterns, construct projects, fit garments, and perform ironing or pressing procedures as well as store supplies. For my business I required room for a desk, computer, filing system, books, and other sources of information. Additionally, I wanted a comfortable area for family and friends to relax in with me and a place for potential clients to sit while in my office.

As you can imagine the result was an unreasonable list of demands which would have been virtually impossible to meet. I didn't get everything I wanted, but the list became a starting point from which I could prioritize my needs from the most to least important. Portions of space could be designated to meet individual needs, while others could "time share."

Without specific expectations, your planning won't be focused and you'll be unable to meet specific needs. A sewer who produces projects for resale has different needs from one who sews fashions for profit or one who sews for enjoyment. A seamstress meeting with clients for consultations and fittings requires a professional businesslike environment. Mass production of projects for resale calls for larger construction and storage areas. There is also the potential for more than one operator to be involved. Sewing for enjoyment means your design space can be based solely on personal requirements.

When designing your space, consider present and future sewing needs. If you feel that two to five years down the road you'll be producing resale products, you need to include that information at the onset of planning.

Even though the style of projects I've sewn varies greatly, the majority of my time is spent producing quilts and clothing. Each of these has separate requirements in terms of space and equipment. As you go through the planning process, keep in mind what types of projects the majority of your sewing time is spent on and what their space requirements are.

1–1. A well-organized sewing space can even be made in a closet. The drop leaf (folded up at left) provides a work surface when lowered (right).

## WHEN WILL YOU SEW?

Although the time frames in which you sew will not affect the actual design of the sewing space, they will have a significant impact on the lighting requirements. If you like to sew during the day and your sewing space has a large, sunny window, you'll have a lot of natural light. If there's relatively little natural light and you sew frequently at just about any time of the day, you'll need to provide additional lighting to reduce eyestrain and minimize errors. Location and lighting sources also influence the color scheme of a room. Light colors will brighten and widen a small, dark area; larger areas with more natural light have significantly different options.

## WHERE SHOULD YOU SET UP YOUR SPACE?

This is probably the most crucial question. Where to sew? Where to set out your myriad personal belongings and develop a haven of creative productivity?

What you want to accomplish will play a large part in your

# PERSONAL PROFILE

## Who Will Work There?

1. Who will be sewing in the space?
2. Is anyone likely to join me there in the future (children, business partner, employees)?
3. Will I ever invite friends over to sew?
4. What is the maximum number of people ever likely to sew there?

## What Will Be Done There?

5. What will I be sewing?
6. What needs do I want my sewing space to meet?
7. What do I see myself sewing 2 to 5 years from now?
8. Will I ever sew professionally?
9. Will I ever sew for resale?

## When Will I Sew?

10. When will I be sewing?
11. Do I intend to sew in the evening?
12. What colors do I want to be surrounded with?

## Where Should I Set Up My Space?

13. Where am I going to sew?
14. What is the size of this area?
15. Is it going to be sufficient for my needs?
16. How much natural light do I have?
17. Is the area well lighted or does it require additional lighting?

## Why Am I Setting Up a Sewing Space?

18. Why am I doing this?
19. What are the additional needs I want my sewing space to meet? (will it function as an office, a child's play area, etc.)

choice of where to sew. Production sewing by several seamstresses requires significantly more space than personal sewing by one individual. If you're fortunate to have a choice of areas, you can do virtually anything. (However, even if you don't have unlimited choices, just about any area can be designed to function more efficiently.) A spare bedroom, the corner of the family room, a hall closet, a stairwell, a section of the garage or the whole garage, a filled-in patio, or a large attic are all areas to be considered. Often it's the less obvious area or the presently useless corner of a room that successfully becomes a functioning and efficient sewing center, frequently without affecting the existing structure of space and family life.

## WHY SET UP A SEWING SPACE?

Why bother getting organized? Who needs a personal sewing space anyway? Why not just dump it all on the kitchen table and eat around it? *Functional*, *productive*, *frustration-free*, *private*, and *professional* are all terms that come to mind when I explain why I need a personal space. Please note I said "explain," not "justify." Many homes have a den or office. Most have a workshop of sorts, even if no one uses the woodworking or mechanical tools much. Many have a two-car garage that stores vehicles and "junk." A sewing room supports the family and nurtures it by providing clothing, warm quilts, and a decorative atmosphere. Home sewing can ease the financial burden of a family or profitably add to the income, while still allowing a parent to remain at home. To productively supply the family, you need an area to work in. To professionally and profitably run a business, you need an office to work from.

Freedom is the greatest derivative of my sewing room: the freedom to be creative, to be surrounded by the "hobby" I love, to run in for ten minutes (when I have it) and quickly sew without pulling out a sewing machine and other supplies and cleaning up each time. This freedom, combined with organization, is what allows you to explore your unlimited creative potential.

Currently, I work a job-share as a receptionist for a large corporation. I get an hour and fifteen minutes for lunch. It takes me seven minutes to drive to and from work, leaving me an hour of uninterrupted time. Seventy-five percent of my lunch hours are spent in my sewing room. To me it's a relaxing hour in the middle of a hectic day.

## HOW CAN YOU CREATE YOUR SPACE?

Want to know how to become more organized, how to design an efficient workspace, how to efficiently lay out a project from start to finish, how to store tools and supplies? Begin by reading the ideas presented in this book. Some will work for you and others won't. But, like friendly advice, take those ideas you like and can use and run with them. The goal here is not for you to duplicate the sewing environment I've created, but to create for yourself one that is efficient, stimulating, and productive.

I've divided the book into two parts. The first one deals with designing and setting up the actual sewing room. We'll start by looking at different sections of the room and the best way to organize them; then you will have a chance to draft your own room. After we've designed the room, we'll look at the available storage space and organize supplies and projects; this is the second part of the book. There is also a chapter on sewing away from home (Chapter 6) and a list of tools (Chapter 7). Some actual, functioning spaces are analyzed in Chapter 8, and shown in full color in the color insert.

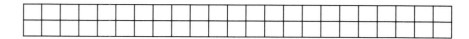

# · 2 ·

# What Am I Doing Here?

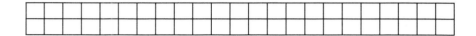

There are five basic functions that have to be performed for virtually any sewing project. Most will require cutting out, stitching, and pressing of fabric at some stage. Alterations may need to be made to the pattern or the garment during fitting. Storage is needed for supplies. Each of these functions is discussed individually in this chapter. Each function has subordinate ones within the greater one. A variety of tools will be mentioned that can be utilized in each area. These tools help alleviate congestion or make the function easier to perform.

## 1. CUTTING AND LAYOUT

### Cutting Surface
A cutting area (Fig. 2–1) will not be of prime importance to

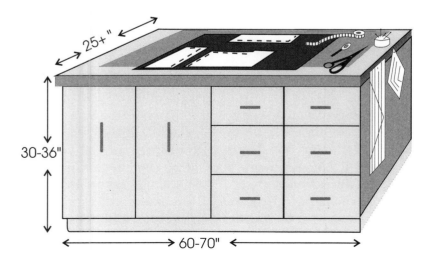

**2–1. Cutting station with tools.**

everyone. However, if your projects require continuous cutting throughout, or if you sew on a production line with other seamstresses, a permanent surface is advisable. One person can cut while another one stitches and another presses.

I find a permanent cutting surface desirable, since it allows me to leave out pattern pieces, fabric, and supplies needed for the various steps of construction while I work back and forth to the sewing machine. Everything is neat, organized, and available, but not in the way of the actual construction. It's extremely frustrating to have supplies that are for the entire project, but that are currently unnecessary, taking up construction space while you're trying to work. The surface should be at least 30″ wide to hold 60″ fabric widths folded lengthwise, but a 36″ width will allow for easier movement of tools, fabric, and pattern pieces around the counter top. A minimum width of 25″ is required to accommodate 45″ widths of fabric, when they are folded (see Fig. 2–1). Most cutting surfaces are 30″ to 36″ high. The correct level depends on your height. You should be able to work easily without excessive bending and back strain or upward arm movement.

As sewing often involves large amounts of fabric, wherever possible construct a surface at least 48″ long, to accommodate fabric for pants or skirt lengths. The maximum surface length is limited by the amount of available room space. With a shorter-length work surface, pattern pieces can be pinned completely to one section of fabric, the fabric can then be rolled up to one side, then the next piece can be pinned, and the fabric rolled some more, and so on until all pieces are in place. These are then cut out following the same process. The majority of work surfaces are between 60″ and 70″ long.

While work surfaces may differ in size, of prime importance is your ability to function within the assigned space. The best arrangement is as an island in the middle of the room, where you can move completely around the unit. This area is similar to a baking island in a kitchen; it is useful for more functions than simply cutting out fabric. However, even if it isn't an island, any clean, accessible work surface simplifies procedures. Add a stool nearby to rest against occasionally. Craft projects such as flower arrangement, making wreaths or baskets, dolls, or stuffed animals (to name a few) can all be created at this wonderful work area.

Several ready-made cutting surfaces are available. I have included illustrations and descriptions of three different types to give you an idea of the broad range of possibilities. Many tables will collapse into smaller units for easy storage. If you don't require a permanent cutting area, if you have limited space, or if you will be moving in the future, consider purchasing one of these collapsible units or constructing something similar.

The 1011T cutting table from Horn of America (Fig. 2–2) is an all-purpose sewing and crafts table. Closed, it's a compact

16″ × 40″. Open, it expands to a flat 72″ × 40″ work surface with a 35″ height. It is both spacious and functional and also easy to close up and store. The utensil and notion bins are useful for small tools and supplies. This is probably one of the more popular styles of ready-made models, as is witnessed by the fact that many companies have a similar version.

Ideal Creations produces the 7010 Craft Mate (Fig. 2–3). With

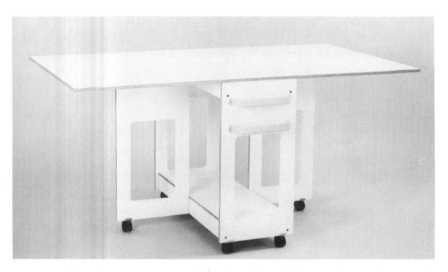

2–2. An all-purpose sewing and crafts table. Photo courtesy of Horn of America.

2–3. A 44½″ × 24″ work table. Photo courtesy of Ideal Creations.

its 24″ depth, 44½″ width and 30″ height, it's slightly small for cutting out sewing projects. However, it provides a great permanent surface in areas of limited space. As its closed size is 24″ × 24″, it can be stored easily to one side. The five drawers add a lot of storage space for cutting tools and other craft and sewing supplies.

Where you absolutely don't have the room but want the benefits of a cutting table, the Sew/Fit Cutting Table might prove to be the answer (Fig. 2–4). This is a cardboard cutting surface that fits together in three pieces. It folds down to a 3″ width for storage. The table has a strong, sturdy surface and measures 34″ high, 32″ wide and 55″ long when open. You can set it up anywhere in just a matter of minutes. Beyond the sewing room, it's ideal to take

**2–4. A folding cardboard cutting surface. Photo courtesy of Sew/Fit Company.**

2–5. A rotary cutting mat. Photo courtesy of Fiskars, Inc.

along to classes or retreats, since often you end up sharing table space in such situations. Having a portable surface has its advantages.

My previous sewing room was small—*minuscule* might be a better word! There definitely was not enough room for anything permanent. Since the laundry room was nearby, I could use the top of the freezer as a cutting surface. It was the right height and big enough for most projects. This is another option when space is limited.

## Cutting Mat and Accessories

Cover the cutting table with a large rotary cutting mat (Fig. 2–5). This is a forgiving surface designed for use with a rotary cutter (Fig. 2–6) and ruler (Fig. 2–7). The mat will protect the surface from being marked by either the rotary cutter or by shears. Having the mat in place keeps it ready for use at any time instead of having to move it up and down. It's also an ideal mat storage solution, since the mats must be kept on a flat surface in order to avoid warping, and they cannot be exposed to excessive heat or sunlight. Many mats have 1″ gridded surfaces for measuring, and numerous sizes of mat are available.

## Bulletin Board

Pin pattern instructions on a bulletin board nearby so you can easily see the next step you need to do without having a bunch of papers cluttering the work surface. Usually this bulletin board will be at or close to the construction surface. If your cutting surface is near a wall, you may want your pattern instructions pinned up there. A piece of plain or fabric-covered corkboard or a sticky board can be hung on the wall to hold this information; or you can purchase 12″ multi-item display tracks; information

2–6. Two sizes of rotary cutters. Photo courtesy of Fiskars, Inc.

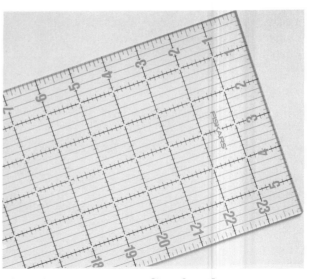

2–7. A transparent acrylic ruler. Photo courtesy of Fiskars, Inc.

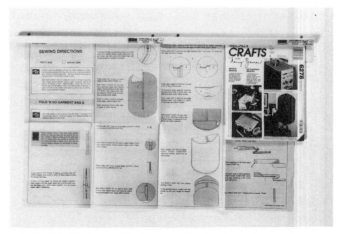

2–8. Multi-item display tracks for hanging pattern instructions. Photo courtesy of Nancy's Notions.

can be inserted into or removed from these tracks easily, without the use of magnets, tacks, or tape (Fig. 2–8). If you hang one at the cutting surface and another in the construction area, it's a simple matter to quickly transfer information from one location to the other.

## Other Tools

Tools kept at the cutting surface should include a rotary cutter, spare blades for the cutter, scissors, rulers, pins and a pinholder, a measuring tape, and markers as well as those for your individual needs. It's important that sharp, potentially dangerous tools such as scissors and rotary cutters be stored safely, especially if small children will be in the sewing area. A scissor block placed in a corner of the cutting surface that children can't reach can store several pairs, keeping them accessible and safe. Perhaps an even safer alternative is to hang these tools up out of reach or to store them in a locked drawer. Rulers can be hung on a suction or cup hook attached to the side of the table. Small baskets or decorative band boxes in place of drawers will hold small tools—but try to stay away from containers that will create clutter instead of eliminating it.

Tools should be contained but they also need to be easily accessible. Hardware, department, and stationery stores carry storage units in all sizes and shapes. They may be designed for one purpose, but are frequently useful for another. Wire baskets that clip under the counter or onto the bottom of overhead shelves are excellent for holding assorted tools. These are traditionally marketed for use in closets or kitchen cupboards, but can be useful at the cutting surface as well as in other areas of the sewing room. Plastic bins, which seem to come in an infinite variety of shapes and sizes, provide a variety of storage solutions.

A magnetic hold-it tray works very well to keep metallic as well as nonmetallic tools together on the surface without spilling (Fig. 2–9). The plastic exterior prevents scratches to counter surfaces, while the magnetic lining secures metallic tools. If you're going to be moving tools from one area to another, a magnetic tray makes the transfer a lot easier.

Rather than running around, back and forth, looking for a tool I just used, moved, or put down somewhere, I like to keep a set of tools in every area, including a measuring tape, thread snipper, pin holder, and pins at the cutting surface, the pressing area, and the construction area. It is expensive to buy that many at once, but if you wait for the sales, you can pick up duplicates over time and the whole sewing experience becomes easier and more functional.

## Waste Fabric

Keep a garbage container close by to dispose of waste fabrics. If you're like me, you save just about any size of fabric scraps that might have another use. However, there are always those pieces that just can't be made into anything else. I use a large, covered container, so scraps aren't disposed of for a couple of weeks. Using this method, I won't throw away a scrap that will suddenly and desperately be required days later. I empty the garbage only after all projects are completed that have some remnants in there; or else I remove scraps that relate to unfinished projects before disposing of the others. Additional garbage containers near the

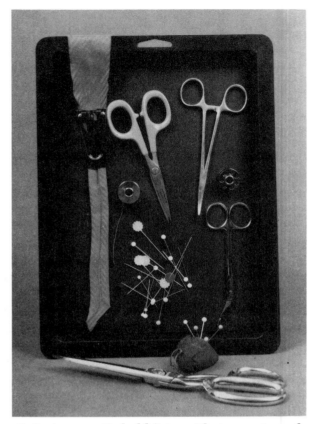

2–9. A magnetic hold-it tray. Photo courtesy of Clotilde, Inc.

construction and pressing areas help to clean up any remaining loose threads. Since garbage cans are available in decorator colors at many department stores, they can be blended into the decor and appear more attractive than functional. Small gift bags are another option; they can easily be set on or attached to the counter to receive small fabric snips and threads. Since the fabric garbage will probably be around for a while, you can see why it's a good idea to reserve these containers for sewing-related scraps only; avoid disposing of food wastes there.

## A Word About Quilting

For producing clothing and crafts, it's nice to have a permanent cutting surface, but it's possible to function relatively well without one if the projects you work on don't require a lot of cutting time. Quilters, on the other hand, especially those using speed-piecing techniques, need a permanent surface. The floor or kitchen counter won't do in this case! These techniques utilize rotary cutters and mats continuously throughout project construction and call for a high degree of accuracy in cutting as well as in stitching. In any circumstance, the availability of a cutting surface will mean a smoother-flowing project. Removing the machine from the counter, replacing the machine, sewing, removing the machine, etc., definitely slows down productivity.

## 2. CONSTRUCTION ZONE

Put on your hard hats; get ready to go! Even though it's easier to have separate areas, the construction zone is one that can be time-shared with the cutting surface. If you have only one work surface, complete as much cutting as possible at one time before replacing the sewing machine on the counter top and beginning to stitch.

There are many ready-made self-contained sewing centers, which are ideal for use in areas with limited space such as a bedroom, hallway, or rec room. These units are attractive, functional, reasonably priced, and available in laminate or wood finishes. Shop around and request brochures from likely sources to see if a unit could meet the requirements of your space. Even if you don't intend to purchase a ready-made unit, the various features available on these units are worth researching and possibly incorporating into your own construction zone. Figures 2–10 through 2–13 show examples of ready-made units.

Another possibility is to get custom-made cabinets, which can be built to your specifications. If you're considering this option, look for a designer who also sews, since she or he will have a better understanding of your wants and needs and can create a workable arrangement for you. Recently I was talking to a saleswoman from a local company who told me about a gorgeous and "absolutely enormous" sewing room she'd just designed. Of course, I was curious to see it and drove 50 miles to view this sure-to-be-delightful space. Though the room was wonderfully done, it could by no stretch of the imagination be considered enormous. It was about the size of an average kitchen eating area. Obviously the saleswoman does not do a lot of sewing!

While custom work surfaces are nice, they're also expensive. You need to be sure the unit will meet your requirements. Folding tables will offer an alternative to ready-made or custom-made surfaces and will give you the opportunity to see how the room layout works before you spend the time and money on other alternatives. They may end up being all you need.

The construction area is composed of two surfaces, one for the sewing machine and one for the serger. Both occupy approximately the same amount of space. Even if you don't already own a serger, design space for one anyway, as the more you sew the more likely the probability of your purchasing this machine. Once your sewing room is designed and in place, you'll

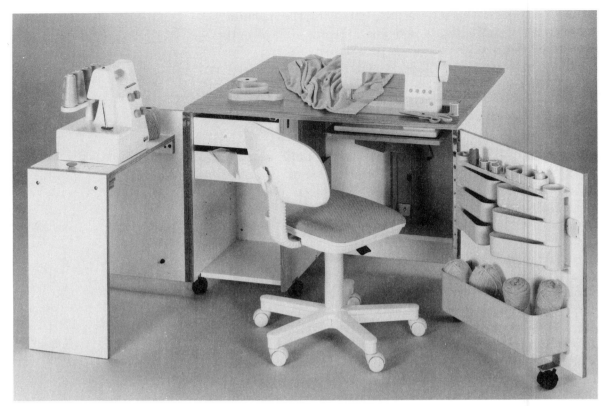

2–10. A modular sewing center, opened up, showing storage and work surfaces. Photo courtesy of Horn of America.

2–11. The modular center shown in Fig. 2–10, closed up. Photo courtesy of Horn of America.

2–12. Another modular sewing center. Photo courtesy of Wood-Tec.

2–13. The modular center shown in Fig. 2–12, closed up. Photo courtesy of Wood-Tec.

find yourself spending a lot more time sewing than before. I'm sure you'll make good use of this "extra" space until it's required. Work surfaces 30″ deep by 60″ long provide a good-sized construction area. If this amount of space isn't available, decrease the measurements (within reason). A minimum of 24″ is necessary for each machine in order to allow you to have enough room for your legs below it, to work comfortably without crowding.

Arrange the units and equipment in a U or L shape (Fig. 2–14). For the U formation, the serger and sewing machine will occupy two of the surfaces, leaving a work space that could function as a cutting or pressing surface, or could simply provide more counter room. If the equipment is set up in an L shape, the machines will be at right angles to each other, making it just a simple quarter-turn from one to the other. An ironing board could be placed along the open side of the L, forming a U. Arrangements such as these best utilize the available space while assuring freedom of movement. When there is more than one seamstress in the sewing center, adjustments need to be made to accommodate both. The U-shape can be set up so that there is a sewing machine on each end and a shared serger in the middle. However, it had better be a wide U to avoid the sewers' constantly bumping into each other. Two separate L shapes could be placed together, forming a T shape, where sewers are facing each other (see Fig. 2–14). The sewing machines would be back to back with sergers at right angles, allowing for easier interaction.

Whether you use custom-made cabinets, portable tables, or shelves to sew on, the bed of the sewing machine should be

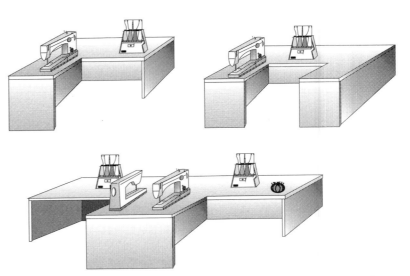

2–14. **Three possible work surface layouts. Top left: L-shaped. Top right: U-shaped. Bottom: T-shape for two sewers.**

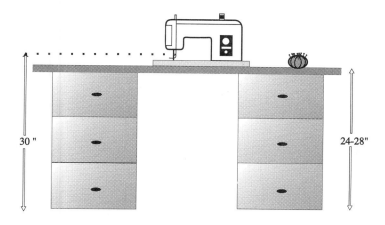

positioned approximately 30″ from the floor (Fig. 2–15). This includes the 2″ to 6″ depth of the machine bed and is considered a "comfortable" working height. Depending on your equipment, the top of the work surface will be between 24″ and 28″ off the floor. This is assuming the machine is set on and not into the counter top. For work on larger projects, or simply for comfort, it is better if the work surface is even with the bed of the machine. The construction surface can either be manufactured to allow the machine to sink into it or an additional surface can be placed around the machine, providing a larger, level bed.

When you are working on a large project that requires greater surface area, remove the serger from the counter and use that surface to support the fabric bulk. If you use only a conventional sewing machine and are working with one construction surface, moving the machine as far to the right of the work surface as possible provides additional counter space. Another solution could be a drop leaf attached to the counter at left of the machine. A fold-down leg would supply additional support so the shelf doesn't bend or fall under the fabric's weight (Fig. 2–16, left). Alternately, a portable extension, kept as an end table in another part of the room when not in use, could be moved next to the machine when needed (Fig. 2–16, right). Bolts attached below the surface of the extension to the fixed cabinet would keep it from shifting and falling.

To avoid fatigue and back discomfort, invest in a proper chair. Next to a sewing machine, this is the most important investment in the sewing room. The chair should be comfortable, adjustable in height, and have a firm backrest for lower back support. Four or five legs versus three will provide a stable base. Look for good quality casters as you'll be moving back and forth a lot, getting up and down and swivelling from one machine to the other. Avoid chairs that have arms. Not only do these get in the way, they catch

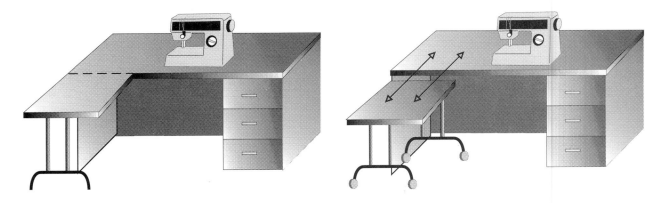

**2–16. Left: a fold-down drop leaf. Right: A portable extension. Both provide extra work space.**

on clothing and cause tears when you get up in a hurry. This is the voice of experience speaking! In one day I ripped both pockets off a sundress! I was more than a little annoyed.

Along with a good chair to preserve back muscles, purchase a pedal support like Neez-Eez and let your knees relax while you sew in comfort (Fig. 2–17). They fit all machine pedals and are tilted so you can avoid that "leaning forward to press the pedal" motion. Such a device is great for marathon sewing sprees.

Office supply stores often carry new and used office furniture and you may be able to purchase equipment at discounted prices. An incredible selection of desks and wall units available are

**2–17. A pedal support eases stress on your knees. Photo courtesy of Clotilde, Inc.**

2–18. A well-organized pegboard can hold most of your construction supplies. Photo courtesy of Nancy's Notions.

adaptable to the sewing environment. Be sure to look at "going out of business" sales for some great deals. Chairs and equipment can be painted or reupholstered to match your decor if they are in poor condition. Along with a chair, a plastic or vinyl mat should be purchased. They're especially useful on carpeted floors. The chair will slide more easily, with less resistance to the flooring, eliminating strain to your leg and back muscles.

Tools used in the construction area can quickly become scattered, creating a messy work surface. They need to be arranged for easy pickup without constantly being in the way. I don't know how many times I've looked for a seam ripper, only to find it's lying on the floor, pushed off the counter by the fabric I'm working with. Pins have the same tendency to drift downward. One of the best solutions for tool organization is pegboard (Fig. 2–18). Paint it to coordinate with the walls to detract from the "out in the garage" ambience, and then mount it near the sewing machine. A large sheet of pegboard equipped with pegs, baskets, small shelves, corkboard, etc., will hold practically all your construction supplies in a neat and orderly fashion.

Drawers are the perfect place for small tools, if your sewing center is equipped with them. If not, a wicker or wire under-counter basket or plastic bins can be used. Whatever the container, it shouldn't be difficult to move and should be large enough for you to replace and remove the tools it holds with ease. If necessary, the wire basket could be lined with decorative fabric to prevent tools from falling through the gaps.

Two items continually clutter up my work surface and I've had to work extra (make that extra, extra!) hard at cleaning them up: pins and thread. A piece of magnetic tape adhered to the flat bed of the machine or the countertop will "catch" pins as they're removed from the fabric. It also will latch onto any other tools containing metal such as thread snippers and seam rippers. (Note: if you've got a computer, don't put a magnetic pin cushion or strip anywhere near it as it will deprogram the computer.) A simple brown lunch bag helped me to deal with my worst habit of throwing loose threads on the floor. Disgusting, isn't it! To beat this I've taped bags to the counter beside the machine and serger to "catch" threads—really close, so they don't have a chance of hitting the floor first. If you don't want to use lunch bags, make a similar product out of fabric, which can be emptied but not thrown away.

## 3. PRESSING

The kind of pressing area needed really depends on the work you do. Garment construction calls for a fairly detailed area as

2-19. Proper position for ironing, in front of ironing board.

Mary Scott operates a home-based cottage industry known as Spectrum Fabricworks Ltd. She manufactures "rainboWear for Kids," a line of colorful, functional, and fun clothing. Mary designs prototypes in this sewing space along with 2 employees, who cut an average of 15,000 articles of clothing per year, and a secretary. The articles are passed on to 13 seamstresses for completion; 15 sales agents work in various capacities to promote the product.

Compare my wish list to the actual room and you'll find I managed to get just about everything I wanted. Desks placed at right angles provide a large construction/cutting area, with the pressing surface completing the U-shape. Pegboards hold an assortment of tools. Out of the picture is a large storage closet. Stools are arranged for the children to color beside me, or for clients. With office and sewing equipment within the same space, it's easy to work back and forth from the design or written text to the actual project.

Described as "absolutely enormous," Becky Drinkwater's sewing room is anything but. However, its curved sewing center, situated just off the kitchen with a great view of the yard and hills beyond, provides a quiet, peaceful and productive sewing space.

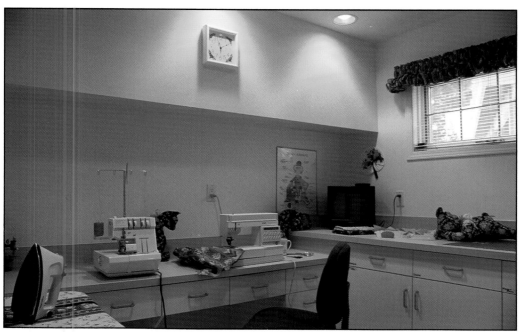

With the placement of her ironing board, construction and cutting/work surfaces, Barb Howell has designed a functional U-shaped sewing center. Recently Barb began producing stuffed animals and crafts for resale. Bulky supplies stored in cupboards below the work area leave the surface clear for cutting, assembling, and finishing products.

Jeanne Chambers, owner of Colonial Crafts, produces a wide array of crafts, from lined baskets and fabric-covered boxes to stuffed animals. Note the storage shelves of fabric, thread, ribbons, lace, and accessories and the pegboard containing various tools and larger items. With its well-organized work spaces, this sewing center is both delightful and functional.

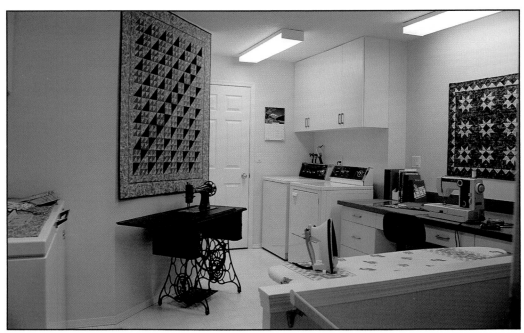

By combining the laundry facilities and sewing requirements, Ruth Goertzen has designed a large sewing center into her home. Because she tends to sew in spurts, she prefers to keep supplies stored and out of sight when not in use. The freezer doubles as a cutting table, with plenty of counter space available for a variety of projects.

pressing is essential to putting life and shape into a garment and creating a professionally finished fashion. Consequently, an extensive array of tools is necessary. Quilting, on the other hand, calls mainly for flat pressing. Less storage space is needed for tools, but a large flat surface is necessary for the long strips, large pieces of fabric and quilt tops.

Some people prefer to remain seated while pressing and incorporate a pressing surface into the construction area, eliminating a lot of jumping up and down. Personally, I prefer to get up and move around a bit. I tend to sew for hours and moving increases blood flow, hopefully utilizes a few calories, and decreases secretarial spread. The pressing surface should be approximately 30″ from the floor if you will be standing to press. If you press while seated, avoid lifting your arms up to reach the equipment. Instead the height should be reached by simply extending the arm with the elbow bent at right angles. This would be the same position used to sew or type. Raise or lower the level of the ironing board to accommodate your body proportions.

Position the equipment so you can press the fabric properly. Your body should be directly in front of the ironing surface. You shouldn't have to twist or lean to perform this function (Fig. 2–19). Positioning your weight incorrectly can place a drag or weight on the iron, causing the fabric to stretch. Instead of just steaming a surface, an incorrect angle may cause you to inadvertently drop the iron on it.

Besides the traditional ironing board (Figs. 2–20, 2–21), several alternative surfaces are available such as countertop (Fig. 2–22), door-mounted, and wall-mounted boards, or ironing blankets. Countertop models are smaller but are easily stored and moved. Door-mounted boards install in virtually no time at all, usually

**2–20. An ironing board with an iron holder. Photo courtesy of Polder, Inc.**

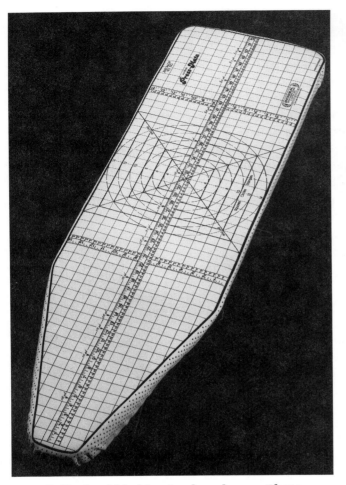

2–21. A gridded ironing board cover. Photo
courtesy of June Tailor, Inc.

2–22. A countertop ironing board. Photo
courtesy of Polder, Inc.

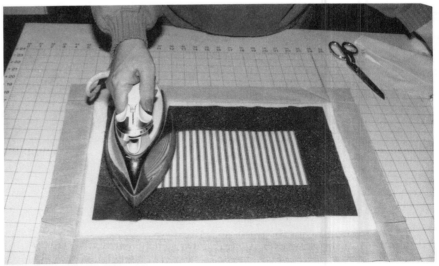

2–23. An ironing surface with grid, Spaceboard. Photo courtesy of
Voster Marketing.

without tools, and are strong and sturdy, holding up to 60 pounds. They fold up and store behind the door when not in use. Wall-mounted boards come with a roll-top front. Attractive as well as functional, they can be used in any multipurpose room without creating an eyesore. An ironing blanket is a portable foam pad with a metallized cover bonded to it. This cover makes it heat reflective, steam permeable and scorch resistant. The blanket can be placed on a flat surface near the sewing machine and be readily accessible for flat pressing. However, since the blanket is soft and foldable, it often shifts on the work surface and needs to be taped in place.

A new board, just recently available, is Spaceboard (Fig. 2–23). Similar to the ironing blanket except with a ¾″ hard core center, its 33″ × 51″ surface is made of heat-resistant materials with a gridded, padded and water-resistant top layer in a heavy-duty gray 100% cotton fabric. The bottom layer is a black polyester feltlike fabric, which prevents the Spaceboard from damaging furniture surfaces; it can also be used for template layout, but it can not be ironed on. The larger board folds in two for easy storage. There's also a smaller, junior version. In addition to being useful in the sewing room, both sizes could be ideal for classroom situations, hotel rooms, dorms, or to take along on the holidays if you like to sew at the campsite! (Occasionally, I must admit that my mind strays from the delightful scenery on a camping trip and wishes for a power generator and my latest project!)

Of all sewing tools, pressing tools are probably the most bulky and difficult to store. Shelving or deep drawers can hold the larger ones such as the dressmakers' ham, seam roll, tailor board, sleeve board, point presser, or clapper (Figs. 2–24 and 2–25). Spray starch or spray bottles plus smaller tools such as a thread snipper, measuring tape, press cloth, and pins can be kept in an ironing board caddy (Fig. 2–26). The caddy screws to the ironing board's surface below the pad. Any weekly ironing supplies will need to be included in the inventory if you'll be ironing finished clothing here also. You shouldn't have to run to the laundry room or kitchen to find something that will be used in the sewing area.

Provide a place to hang projects after pressing to avoid rewrinkling them. Most of us don't enjoy ironing enough to do it more often than we have to. When there isn't a closet available, a piece of wood dowelling or a shower rod suspended from the ceiling will work. Wall hooks will also provide hanging space, or an ironing board rack like Handy Hanger can be attached to the ironing board (Fig. 2–27). This rack slips over the wide end of the ironing board, providing a convenient place to hang garments before and after pressing. Whatever your options, create sufficient space to avoid overloading and crushing garments together.

**2–24.** An assortment of pressing tools, including dressmakers' hams, seam roll, sleeveboard, ham stands, and an iron. Photo courtesy of June Tailor, Inc.

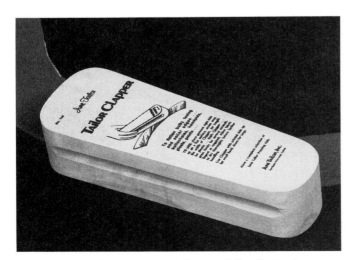

**2–25.** A clapper, a pressing tool for flattening seams. Photo courtesy of June Tailor, Inc.

**2–26.** An ironing board caddy can hold small pressing tools. Photo courtesy of Mildred's Winning Combinations.

2–27. An ironing board with a Handy Hanger rack. Photo courtesy of American Homeware.

You also want to insure that the flooring won't tire your feet, especially if you'll be pressing for a lengthy period of time. A mat thrown over a spongy surface or foam surface will give extra resilience to a hard floor. If you're working on a cement surface, it will also keep your feet from getting too cold.

## 4. FITTING AND ALTERATIONS

In some cases, an area for fittings and alterations may not be necessary. If you produce craft items, but no garments, you probably won't need a mirror, hem guide, or fitting tools. (Unless you're fitting for the Teddy Bear Tea or the Bunny Rabbit Picnic!) However, if you're a professional seamstress with clients coming into the home for fittings, this area is critically important.

Any adjustments should be made to the pattern before you begin a project. Excess pattern tissue or tissue paper can be used to alter patterns. I usually trace out each separate size from multisized children's patterns. I don't always have tissue paper

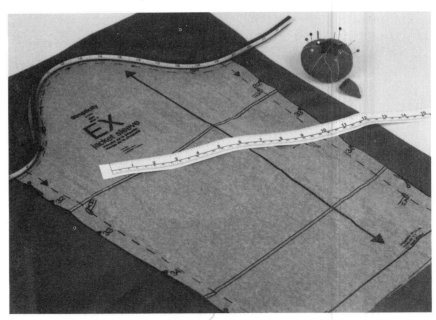

2–28. A flexible ruler measures curved lines. Photo courtesy of Clotilde, Inc.

around, so I use wax paper and a small felt-tip pen. Because of the space it provides, you'll most likely make these adjustments at the cutting surface. If you store tissue or wax paper there—as well as index cards, markers, scotch tape, and a pen—you'll avoid running to the kitchen and riffling through the "junk" drawer every time you have a few changes to make. (You'll also be kept from passing by the refrigerator and being lured into its depths!)

For taking measurements and making adjustments along curved edges, use a flexible ruler like Flexible Curve (Fig. 2–28). It holds its shape and measurements while you bend it around curved edges like sleeve caps and necklines to get accurate measurements. Note any adjustments you've made to a pattern on an index card and staple it to the instruction sheet. Date the card so you can easily see when the pattern was last used and will know if it requires further adjustments. Anyone else using the pattern will be immediately alerted that changes have been made to the original sizing.

After you've altered a pattern and cut and sewn the main pieces together, you'll want to fit the garment. Whether you fit it to yourself, another person, or to a dress form, a mirror is essential to view the hang of the garment and see where any further adjustments need to be made. Mount a full-length mirror in a location that provides enough distance for the person to stand back and view his or her entire figure. The back of a door is often the perfect location, since the door will be closed for privacy during the fitting.

Privacy is especially important when fitting customers. The

room must at least have a door and if possible provide a small changing cubicle. No matter how good a seamstress you are, unless customers feel comfortable and inconspicuous while being fitted, they won't request future work.

Pins are the main tool for fittings. Store them with a pinholder, measuring tape, and various styles of shoulder pads in a small basket near the mirror (Fig. 2–29). A half-basket mounted against the wall will keep supplies out from underfoot but within reach if you're fitting yourself, though a smaller movable basket may be easier for fitting clients.

A hem marker is invaluable in achieving an even hem (Fig. 2–30). They're available in several different models, some of which can be operated by the person trying on the garment. However, I find the most accurate is the pin type. You'll need help, but it's so easy someone else can give you a hand, even a child, and it is very accurate.

What about quilt fittings? While not "fitted" as we traditionally think of the term, quilts require designing space. I use a large flannel board to place quilt blocks and get the overall effect of the quilt before I sew it together (see color insert, page B). You get a

**2–29. A fitting area.**

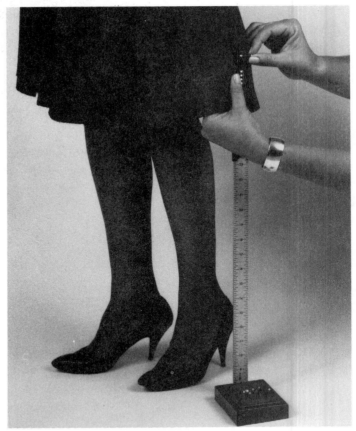

2–30. Using a hem marker. Photo courtesy of Clotilde, Inc.

more realistic impression with the blocks up against the wall than looking down at them flat on the floor or on a bed. Flannelette or craft batting mounted on the wall or stapled around a piece of plywood works very well for this purpose.

## 5. STORAGE

Another consideration is storage. When I mentioned this area of my book to a friend her comment was, "Storage! What's to it? Just store it." I used to relate to that thought. It was my habit to grab the nearest box, stuff everything in and throw it on the shelf. Out of sight, out of mind! Unfortunately, it didn't work too well. When I needed something later, I would have to pull down every box and look through it to discover if this was the place I had packed away long-lost item X.

While storage is one of the five functions of the sewing area, it's a complex and diverse one that requires special considerations. Storage for required supplies is a big part of sewing and for that reason I'm going to deal with it in a separate chapter (Chapter 4).

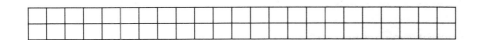

## · 3 ·

# Designing the Layout

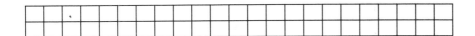

Now, after much discussion, we're ready to design your sewing room. Review the Personal Profile Chart in Chapter 1 (page 14) to refamiliarize yourself with your personal requirements. As you design, keep in mind the five functions commonly performed in most sewing studios, as well as any additional ones specific to your situation:

1. Cutting and layout
2. Construction
3. Pressing
4. Fitting and alterations
5. Storage

You'll need some graph paper, a sharp pencil, an eraser, a metal or wooden measuring tape and a ruler to plot the design. Use a ruler to draw neat, clean, straight lines. You'll find this makes the diagram easier to follow. Completely erase any incorrect lines when making changes.

## 1. DESIGNING THE FLOOR PLAN

Start drafting the basic floor plan by measuring the perimeter of the room. Since you need accurate measurements, it might be easier to have someone help you. Using ¼″ graph paper, with a scale of one square equals one foot (¼″ = 1′), draft the outer measurements onto the paper. This is your floor plan. An example of a floor plan is shown in Fig. 3–1.

Along with the outer measurements, accurately plot the location of windows, closet openings and doorways. Show which way the door opens. Show any irregularities in wall shaping or

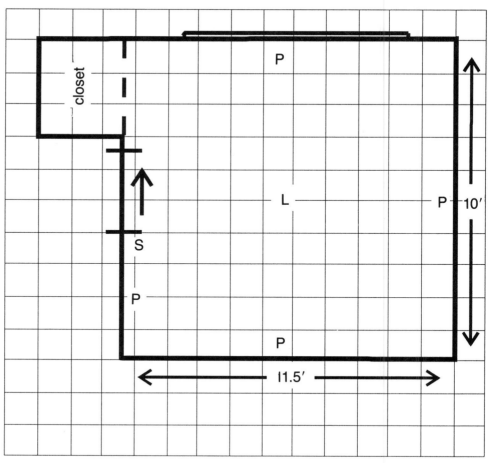

**3–1. Sample floor plan showing closet, outlets along the floor (P), and light fixtures (L).**

architectural objects (these are those annoying little ducts and drains that the builder inconveniently arranged in the middle of the room or allowed to jut out of the wall). Sometimes, when you're not used to working from a floor plan, it also helps to draw a plan of each wall, noting the location of windows, closet openings, doorways, and other irregular features. This plan will show more clearly how far off the floor these features are located and will assist in the placement of equipment as well as shelving, pegboard, lighting, and other overhead fixtures. Other examples of floor plans are given later in this book.

## 2. ELECTRICAL OUTLETS

Since you're only working with a floor plan, nothing permanent has been built into the room yet. This is the time to make sure that sufficient electrical outlets are available and correctly positioned. Mark the placement of outlets on the floor plan. We could use a bunch of technical symbols here, but it's just as easy to use a P for plug-ins along the floor and PC for those at counter height. Are there enough outlets? Are they in the correct positions or are they covered by counters and cupboards? You will probably find that additional outlets are required, possibly even a separate circuit. Sewing machines require very little electricity, but heating equipment consumes a lot.

Electrical safety codes differ from region to region. If you're doing any rewiring, be sure and contact a qualified electrician for advice. Any wiring that is done must meet the electrical code requirements and be approved by the local electrical inspector. In the case where a sewing studio is being designed and built from "scratch," the location of electrical outlets will be designated after the room design is complete, but it's also possible to provide for additional electrical needs within an existing space.

The style and number of electrical outlets needed depends on the number of persons operating in the room and the equipment being used. Each piece of equipment should contain a label with the electrical power rating on it. Most sewing machines are 100 watts and irons typically are 1,200 watts. A standard electrical circuit supplies up to 1,500 watts safely. After this point, the circuit may become overloaded. Consider using two circuits with split receptacles. Split duplex receptacles are most commonly used in kitchens. The top and bottom outlets, within one receptacle, are separated to different circuits. If two high-wattage appliances are connected to the outlet, the circuit will not become overloaded.

Electrical cords across the surface of a counter are exposed to damage from sharp scissors, rotary cutters, seam rippers, and pins. Locate electrical outlets below the counter surface and drill holes in the counter top to feed the cord through. These drilled holes would be similar to those used in office equipment for computers. Use tape or hooks below the counter surface to keep the cords from dangling down and tangling with your feet. As it creates a safety hazard, avoid stretching extension cords across the room. If a cord is necessary, purchase one that is long enough to run around the room, following the outer wall. Tuck the cord under the baseboard, or use tape, adhesive clips, or nail-on clips to keep it out of the way. The cord should be in good shape— no nicks, cuts, or exposed wires. Extension cords with three conductors and three-prong ends should always be used with equipment that has a three-prong plug. If cords need to run along the counter or floor, use cord covers to protect them.

Power bars will provide extra outlets. These are considered safe, though you should choose one with a built in circuit breaker to provide additional protection against circuit overloading.

Another alternative to electrical outlets is a power track. Power tracks are located above counter level around the outer perimeters of the room. It is a long track that supports movable outlets. The wire within the track is shielded, well hidden, and not directly exposed. This electrical system is ideal in classroom situations or where there is more than one seamstress, or when equipment is frequently moved.

## 3. LIGHTING

Note the location of any permanent light fixtures as well as wall switches on the floor plan. A simple L can be used to designate a permanent light fixture or one that is wired in and the symbol S can indicate wall switches.

General, direct, and task lighting are all required for a comfortable working environment and to avoid eye strain. The primary light fixture should provide a high level of overall illumination. Fluorescent lighting is considered the best choice for this purpose. It provides an efficient and bright light and is cooler than heat-generating incandescent bulbs.

Because your body is between the main light source and the work surface, a large portion of light is blocked. Direct lighting will eliminate shadows on or around the work surface. Consider mounting fluorescent lights under overhead shelves or on the wall above the work space. Fluorescent tubing can be concealed with a 3″ or wider strip of wood.

While general and direct lighting are the first requirements of the room, specific task lighting should also be considered, especially for any hand stitching. Clip-on or gooseneck lamps are ideal, since they can be positioned correctly while you work and then can be removed when no longer in use. The bulb should be located 12″ to the side of the work, 7″ behind it, and 14″ to 15″ above it. Most clip-on or gooseneck fixtures have a maximum rating of 60 watts. Bulbs with a wattage higher than 60 to 100 are not recommended for task lighting. Not only would they be a poor light source, they're tremendous heat generators. Halogen lighting is an alternative. Small halogen lights generate a very bright, intense, directional light, and many fixtures can be purchased with a light intensity control. However, halogen lighting gets extremely hot, so it isn't usable for any length of time.

Take into account the color of walls, ceiling, cabinets, and carpet. Light is absorbed by dark colors and reflected by lighter ones. Twice as much light is required in a room with dark walls, floors or counter tops. Even the window treatments can affect the light. Light treatments reflect light and dark ones cut it. Each room has its own lighting needs and problem areas. Seek the advice of a specialist at a lighting shop, who can advise on the number, size, and placement of lights for your particular requirements.

## 4. FURNITURE PLACEMENT AND TRAFFIC FLOWS

We've already talked a lot about the requirements of each area of the sewing room and noted that there are several alternatives. Unless you're anticipating moving in the relatively near future, you may find that custom cabinets are the best option, since they can provide exactly what you want at a price similar to ready-made ones. Because they are built in they have the advantage of being very stable, resulting in vibration-free sewing.

Various styles, arrangements and storage solutions are available from kitchen/bath companies, but basically there are two types of cabinets to choose from: custom-made and modular, which are designed for kitchen, bathroom, and desk functions. Custom-made cabinets are made to any specification required, with accessory options. Modular units are less expensive since they are mass produced, but have the disadvantage of being available only in specific depths and heights. They are usually produced as follows:

*Kitchen:* Base cabinets have a standard depth of 24″, height of 36″ including counter top, and widths ranging from 9″ to 48″ (usually in 3″ increments). Wall cabinets have the same range of widths and are 12″ deep and 12″ to 42″ high. Taller units, extending from the floor to ceiling, are 12″ to 42″ wide, 12″ to 24″ deep, and 84″ to 96″ high.

*Bathroom:* Since a mirror is usually mounted above a bathroom cabinet, they're available in base units only. The range of sizes available are widths of 12″ to 48″, depths of 18″ to 21″, and heights of 32″ to 33″, including counter top.

*Desk:* Not all modular cabinet companies offer these units, since they are specific to desk requirements with widths of 12″ to 30″, a depth of 24″, and height of 30″ including the counter top. While they may work for a cutting area, since the height and depth of the modular units is predetermined, desks are often the incorrect size for a specific function. Usually the counter is too high for comfort while sewing. You can alter the height of the unit by cutting 2″ off the 4″ toe kick. This leaves a remaining 2″ which is still sufficient toe space when standing close to the cabinets. Another solution is to use the modular units for storage or pressing areas, but build a separate counter top for the construction area, dropping it to the required height.

It's quite easy to increase the depth of the units by setting them

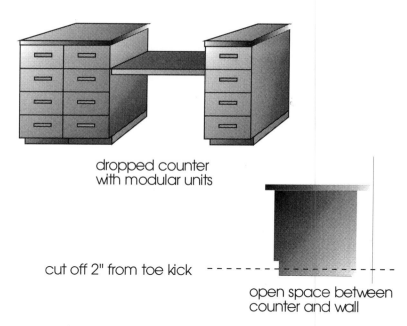

dropped counter
with modular units

cut off 2" from toe kick

open space between
counter and wall

**3–2. Dropping a counter top to suit a sewer.**

forward from the wall the required distance and then
constructing the counter top to reach the entire depth. While the
cabinet might be only 18″ in depth, the counter top can be 30″ if
desired. Since it's cleated to the wall, it's quite secure (Fig. 3–2). A
spacer can be used to fill in the gap between the back of the
cabinets and the wall, hiding any unsightly and dust-collecting
"holes" behind the cupboards.

Although a custom cabinet company will measure and draft the
room and probably offer a variety of arrangements to you, you
should still draft out the room to help formulate some ideas of
your own ahead of time and get an impression of the traffic flows.
The designer can then work on the final layout and, between the
two of you, any problem areas can be discussed and solved.
Sometimes a room looks quite big and full of possibilities until
you draft in the cabinets and find that while everything fits there's
only about 6″ between the units. Since this isn't enough space to
squeeze most adult bodies through, some changes have to be
made!

Collect sample brochures of furniture. Make sure the
furniture's size specifications are given. After you've collected
information on all the products you intend to include in the room,
furniture and equipment placement can be decided. If you intend
to include a piece of equipment at a later date, get its
measurements now and work it into the floor plan. Otherwise, you
may be disappointed to find it won't fit in. Even if you're using
custom cabinets, some equipment will still need to be purchased.
Measure the cutting table, sewing center, ironing board, chair,

and any portable tables. Treat a cubicle for fittings and a mirror as you would a furniture piece and measure it for proper placement. You need the height, width, and depth of each piece. Using the same ¼″ scale as you used for the room, plot the shapes of all furniture and other space-consuming items onto graph paper and cut each one out (Fig. 3–3) as a template. Measure and cut out templates for the cutting, construction, and pressing surfaces also. Templates should be made not only for the floor plan but also for the wall plan (see Fig. 3–3, right). Draw a template equal to the width and depth or floor size of each item and another equal to the height and width or wall size. Label them and cut them out.

When arranging the templates on the floor and wall plans, allow space for movement around each. The construction area must include enough space to move and get into and out of the chair. Allow 2′ away from the construction surface for a chair to be pulled back and sat on. Movement around the room shouldn't be restricted by furniture or tools jutting into the main traffic flow. Don't place shelves, hooks, or rods in overhead locations that could prove dangerous. Be safety-conscious! A 4′ to 5′ width is

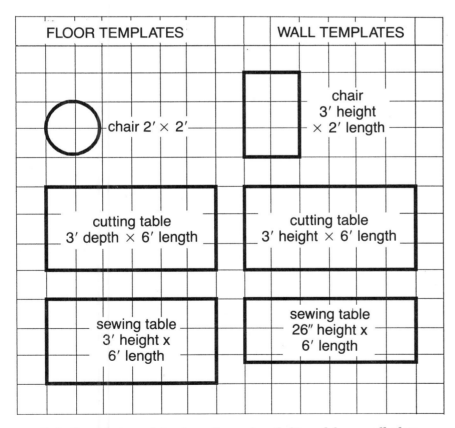

**3–3. Sample templates for a floor plan (left) and for a wall plan (right) show the same three pieces of furniture diagrammed from above (left) and from a side view (right).**

required for major traffic patterns; an 18″ width is required for minor ones. Since most sewing rooms don't have a major traffic lane through them, a width of 30″ to 36″ is sufficient. If you're occupying a narrow room or galley, the larger width will be necessary. A work island requires a 36″ pathway for people to move around it without shuffling sideways or bumping into things. If one side of the island is by a wall and not next to another counter, an 18″ pathway is sufficient, unless there are storage units along the wall, in which case you'll require the wider pathway. A 36″ space is needed for ease of standing in front of opening drawers. Space requirements for the pressing area will differ, depending on the style of surface you are working with.

Keeping ease of movement in mind, shift the templates around the floor plan and wall plan until you achieve the most workable placement. Don't rush the final decision. Instead, arrange several options and think about and analyze them carefully for several days. Keeping in mind that this is your room and that in the end it must work for you, gather opinions. Someone else may see a problem you hadn't noted before. Because of lack of space or the location of architectural features, some compromises will have to be made. Take the time to make sure you've covered as many angles as possible and have achieved the best solution. Once the correct furniture placement has been decided on, draw the furniture onto the floor and wall plans.

Now look at the remaining areas in terms of storage. Pegboard, corkboard, overhead shelves, etc., need to be positioned for easy access without being in the way. Is there sufficient storage or will more be required? Diagram any closets for shelving and hanging requirements. Look at under-counter space and decide where drawers and cupboards should be located. An opening at least 2′ wide is needed below each machine to provide enough free space for knees and feet. Draw all these features onto the wall plan also.

## 5. WALLS AND FLOORS

Of the options available for wall treatments, paint is the cheapest and easiest to change at a later date. It's also easy to keep clean if you choose paints that are washable. Stencilling, murals, and graphics will add interest, as will wallpaper. Not only will wallpaper hide any wall inconsistencies, it adds pattern, texture and design to the walls. Light colors and patterns will reflect light better than dark ones.

Options for flooring include vinyl, hardwood, carpet, and tile. Discount tile immediately if you'll be standing for any length of time as it's very hard to stand on and difficult to keep clean. Antifatigue mats can be purchased to help relieve leg and back strain resulting from hard flooring surfaces. Hardwood floors are very attractive but require considerable upkeep. They can become scratched and damaged by casters and sharp objects such as dropped pins, shears, or rotary cutters. Carpeting is warm and comfortable. Choose a low, dense pile to avoid snagging pins and to make rolling chairs easier. Check out samples before purchasing carpet by rolling a chair on them and by dropping pins into them to see how easily they are retrieved. Vinyl floors are the least expensive. Stick to a medium value as lighter colors are more apt to show dirt and darker ones absorb light. Flooring is available in numerous designs, qualities, and styles. Consult with a flooring specialist on which choice is the most suitable.

## 6. EXAMPLES OF FLOOR PLANS

Some floor plans and their corresponding three-dimensional drawings of sample layouts are illustrated here to give you an indication of how cabinetry could be arranged (Figs. 3–4 to 3–11). The four basic shapes are a one-wall, L-shaped, U-shaped, and island floor plan. The diagrams don't include all the little details we've been talking about in terms of pegboard, notions, etc., but are more general, to give you a feel for the possibilities. How you arrange tools and shelving really depends on the available wall space, closets, windows, and other architectural features in your room.

## 7. THE FINISHING TOUCHES

The basic requirements of the sewing space have been met. You have chosen the arrangement of furniture and equipment and are now ready to complete the room. Recheck your floor plan and wall diagrams before beginning any work. Check for adequate electrical outlets and lighting requirements, for correct traffic flow and ease of movement, and to be sure that you've included space for the various functions. Measurements for special orders such as shelving, counters and cupboards, flooring or window treatments should be taken by the manufacturer. This isn't to say that your measurements aren't accurate—it simply protects you if something doesn't fit correctly.

When the design is complete, the work can begin. This is your space that is being created. It should function efficiently and provide for all your production requirements, but it also should be a space that reflects your personality, creativity, and lifestyle. Choose fabric, colors, and textures that appeal to you. And, above all else, have fun!

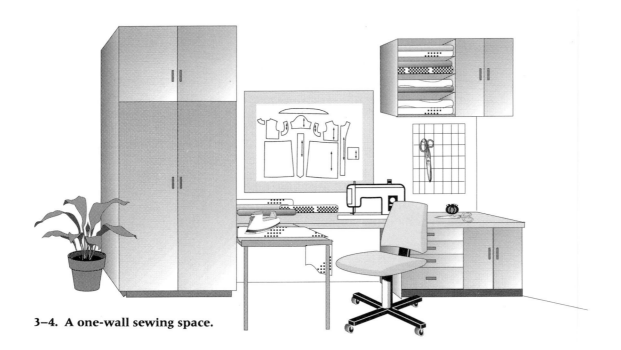

3-4. A one-wall sewing space.

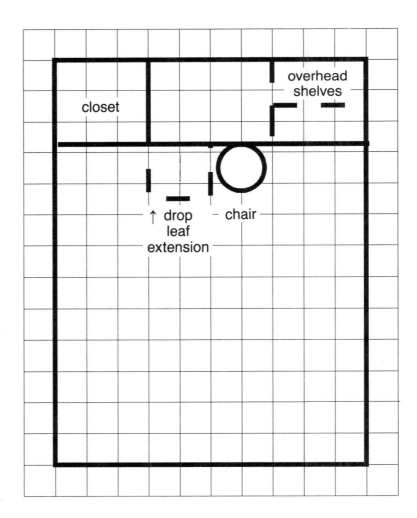

3-5. A floor plan of the sewing space
shown in Fig. 3-4.

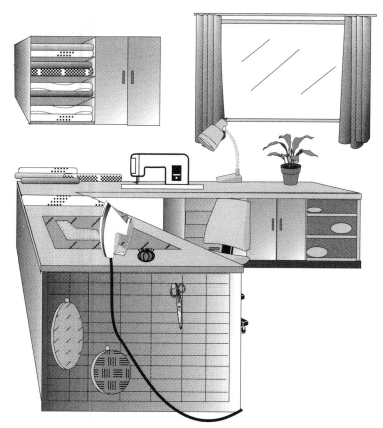

3–6. An L-shaped sewing space.

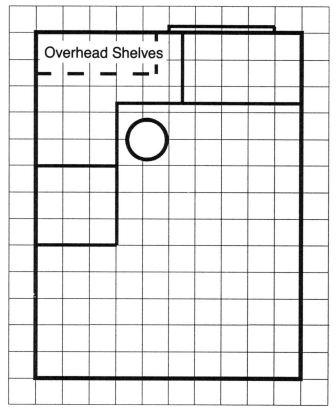

Overhead Shelves

3–7. A floor plan of the L-shaped space shown
in Fig. 3–6.

3–8. A U-shaped sewing space.

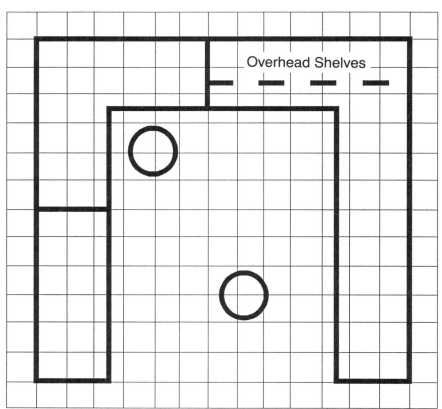

Overhead Shelves

3–9. A floor plan of the U-shaped sewing space shown in Fig. 3–8.

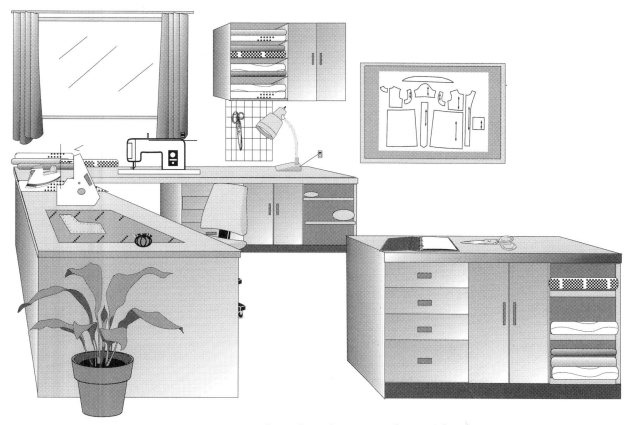

3–10. An L-shaped sewing space plus an island.

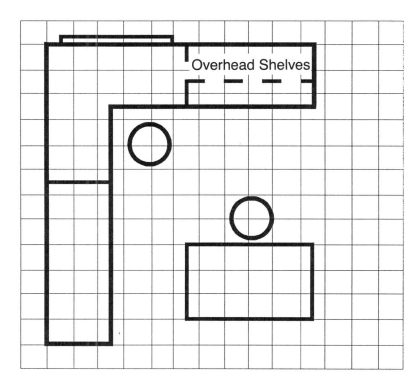

Overhead Shelves

3–11. A floor plan of the L-shape plus island sewing space shown in Fig. 3–10.

# PART TWO

# Organizing Supplies and Projects

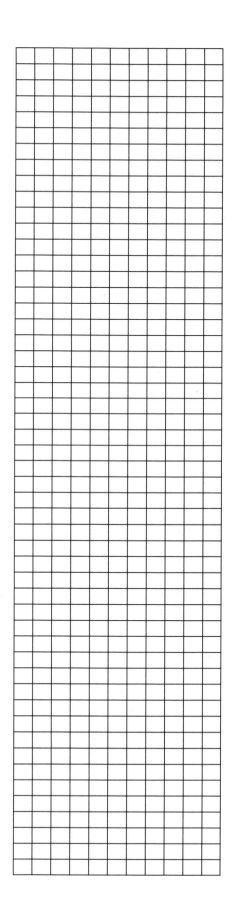

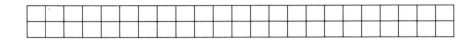

# · 4 ·

# Storage: Know What You Have and Where to Find It

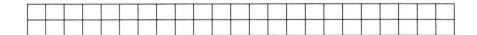

Let's face it, sewing requires a lot of tools, notions, information and equipment. The more involved you become, the more you acquire. How does the saying go? "She who has the most fabric when she dies wins." I don't know about you, but I am definitely in the race! All those supplies we acquire need to be stored properly so we can find them later. From the options available, a system can be customized to suit your requirements. The amount of available space and the extent to which you sew will factor into the plan and affect the overall design. There's no use planning for options that simply don't apply to you. So, once again, you don't want to exactly copy my system, but take from it useful ideas and design your own. Although it takes time to set any system in place, I would encourage you to get started as soon as possible. After the initial setup, you'll find it works well and is easy to maintain.

Begin this step of your room design by thoroughly sorting your supplies and eliminating anything that's no longer required. Sort the supplies into three categories: those to be disposed of, those that belong in another room, and those you definitely want to keep. Be ruthless! If you've never used an item, never intend to use it, and see no purpose for it, get rid of it. This includes your fabric supplies. If you have fabrics that haven't been looked at in the last two years, are hopelessly out of date, and will never be used, get rid of them! Gasp! Did she say get rid of them? Remember I was referring to out-of-date or unusable fabrics. Don't panic! Any "usable scraps" of fabric should be saved for those times when little bits of one color or texture are required.

Just be sure that what you're saving is really worthwhile. I approached my fabrics rather ruthlessly the other day and weeded out two grocery bags full of what I had once deemed to be usable amounts of fabric. At second glance, they had no real purpose unless I intended to produce miniatures—which I don't! (P.S.: If you really can't bear to part with anything, cut the fabric scraps into small strips or pieces and use them as stuffing for pillows or small animals.)

Unnecessary supplies can sometimes be used by friends, given to charities, or sold at garage and craft sales. You know the saying: "One man's junk is another man's treasure." Children love to build collages with fabrics and trims. Avoid throwing away any scraps by giving them to a preschool or kindergarten class. They are always looking for good "stuff" to make art projects out of and will make wonderful use of these "treasures."

Remove everything from the storage area except those supplies that relate directly to your sewing space. These will be used to set up the initial storage system. You'll need a few storage containers to get started. They can be purchased either from stationery stores or department and photography shops. But please finish reading this entire chapter before rushing out to buy anything. Make notes on what supplies you have to store, the amount of space available, the method to be used, and the appropriate-sized containers needed before purchasing anything, so you don't end up with a lot of supplies that aren't going to work for you. Some storage supplies you probably will need are:

1. Boxes
2. Index cards and plastic pouches to put them in (choose ones that are sticky on three sides)
3. $3\frac{1}{2}'' \times 5''$ and $8'' \times 10''$ photograph album pages (the transparent kind)
4. Three-ring binders to fit the photo album pages
5. Marking pens

Throughout this chapter, various supplies that are commonly stored in a sewing room will be discussed. These are the more common ones that require larger amounts of storage space; in all probability you'll have others. Based on the system outlined, however, the others can be stored as efficiently as any discussed here.

## 1. BOXES

Before I begin any further explanations, let's talk about boxes. Not too exciting, but critical! Large cardboard boxes are the best

**4–1. Cardboard boxes with lids are good for storing supplies like fabric. (Yours will not require the folders inside shown in this photo, however.) Photo courtesy of Fellowes Manufacturing.**

storage containers. The large ones that I use for fabric storage are 18″ × 13″ × 10″ and can be purchased at a stationery or department store (see Fig. 4–1). Photocopy paper comes in similar boxes; an office may be able to provide you with some from their photocopy department. The boxes you use must all be the same size. Avoid boxes that have a lot of writing on them; look for ones that come with lids instead of fold-down flaps. Inserting and removing supplies is much easier if you don't have to refold the flaps every time you remove an item or return it.

If you'd prefer to use plastic boxes instead of the cardboard ones, make sure the lids are easy to remove and that they will stack well. I don't recommend plastic for fabric supplies, because the fabric can't breathe properly and can become discolored, subject to mildew, and generally worn down. If you have a lot of fabric, some may need to be stored for quite a long time.

Now, after saying that the boxes must all be the same size, that doesn't mean *all* of them are the same size. What I am saying is: don't collect an assortment of boxes where no two are alike. The boxes for large storage items should be one size, for patterns another size, and for small notions another size, etc. If you have more than three to four different sizes of boxes, you have too many and things will get complicated when it comes to storing them.

Consider purchasing pattern boxes (Fig. 4–2 and 4–9). These are smaller decorative boxes that will contain a variety of supplies besides patterns and will store more easily than large ones in a

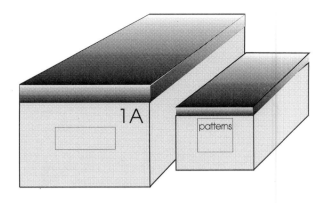

**4–2. Left: a fabric storage box. Right: a pattern box.**

confined space. They're especially wonderful if you're storing some supplies in the sewing area and some in a utility room farther away.

Attach a plastic pouch to the outside of each box. The contents of the box will be listed on an index card which is then slipped into the pouch. Never write this information directly on the box. When the contents of the box change, you simply change the index card. Everything is neat and clean without a lot of scribbling on the outside of the box to cause confusion as to what's really in there (Fig. 4–3). As the pattern and fabric boxes are filled with supplies, use a marking pen to label each box numerically in the top right-hand corner. If a similar item is contained in more than one box, use an alphanumerical sequence. For example, if you have three boxes of fabrics you could number them 1A, 1B and 1C (see Figure 4–2).

The index cards are there to tell you what is in each box. However, even though it's a lot easier than searching through the entire contents of the room, you're not going to want to read every one to find what you're looking for. As we set up the system, a cross-reference system will be created: sources such as the Fabric Filing System and pattern catalogues (explained later in this chapter) will indicate which box to look in for a particular supply. Why bother with the index cards outside the boxes then? They're there so you don't have to search the reference files to find out what's in a specific box. You can quickly read the index card. This is very helpful if the boxes are in the garage and the list is at the sewing center. The cross-reference simplifies everything and saves time and energy for being creative. (If you're feeling a little bit in the dark, relax. The system will become clearer as we discuss the different items being stored.)

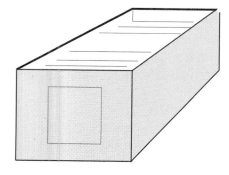

4–3. Left: A pattern storage box. Right: A pattern envelope photocopied on looseleaf paper (front and back).

## 2. THE STORAGE AREA

As you begin sorting and arranging your supplies into boxes, you'll need to have a storage area in mind. Experienced interior decorators recommend that 10% to 15% of the home be used for storage. Applying this ratio to the sewing room, carefully analyze the wall space above, below, and around the sewing center. When designing the room, you probably designated some storage areas, but there may be more space to build additional storage than you first imagined. Any unclaimed length of wall is potentially available for storage. Shelves built into a closet will keep supplies accessible but not visible. Under the sewing counter is another prime spot. Above counters, under stairs, the laundry room, the spare-room closet, and the garage are all alternate areas.

If there isn't room for storage containers in the sewing area, separate the items to store nearby from the ones that can be farther away. Running out to the garage every time you need some interfacing or a button won't be too productive. Keep small, frequently used notions close to the construction area and others, such as patterns and fabric, which are not used continuously, farther away.

Some people like their supplies on open shelves where they can see everything quickly without opening and closing cupboard doors. Others like them tucked away out of sight. If you prefer not to have supplies on display, purchase cabinets with doors, or make decorative curtains to cover shelves. Economical ready-made shelving units are available from most home supply stores and can be easily assembled. Office furniture also offers a variety of solutions.

Many how-to books on building storage units have been published. These allow you to have the look and sizing of custom cabinetry without the expense. Even though I'm not too handy with wood and a hammer, I've considered building my own units. Think positively! If you're skilled in this area or know someone who is, it's definitely a viable option. I've been told that shelving units are fairly basic to build.

## 3. FABRIC

For the majority of us, the main item to be stored is fabric. I use both fashion and quilting fabrics. Since I can't seem to walk by a fabric store without acquiring a new piece of yardage, I have a lot of fabric to store.

A resolution I once made was to use the fabric I had on hand before purchasing more. The theory was that I would check my existing supplies to see if I had anything appropriate before rushing out and buying something first. Sounds good until you try to put it into practice. If you aren't organized, endless hours are spent sifting through the same fabric piles over and over because you don't really know what you have or how much of it. This is frustrating. All you want to do is sew. Before you know it, you're back at the store buying another piece of fabric and justifying your actions by assuring yourself that for the next project you'll take the time to sort. Right now, you're in a hurry! However, I was always in a hurry and I never got around to using up those fabrics. Consequently many become outdated and unusable. My Fabric Filing System is the result of a lack of time and a lack of willingness to sort every time I wanted to begin a new project.

As you've probably gathered, I like to sew whenever I have a minute. I don't like to be slowed down by little tasks that could be done in advance, such as pretreating fabric. To get around this, I pretreat yardage when it arrives home from the store. Then I know that all the fabrics in my storage boxes have been pretreated and are ready to cut out. It really doesn't matter if you prewash the fabric when you store it or just before cutting it out. It's your personal choice. However, I would recommend following one system or the other consistently to avoid confusion. If you don't use a fabric for several years and don't have a consistent system, you'll be wondering whether it has or hasn't been prewashed.

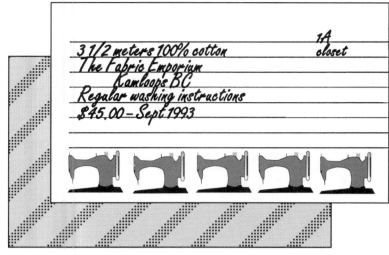

**4–4. A fabric index card, indicating various details including the fabric box** *(1A)* **and location** *(closet)* **of the stored fabric.**

The handwritten card reads:

3 1/2 meters 100% cotton
The Fabric Emporium
Kamloops BC
Regular washing instructions
$45.00 – Sept. 1993

1A
closet

After pretreating and before storing the fabric, clip a small corner off one end. While I've recommended pretreating all fabric before storing, this system will identify whether or not a fabric has been processed. (Unprocessed fabrics won't have the clip mark.) You may be planning to use the fabric right away, but if it takes a little longer to get going, this system will ensure that stored fabrics can be easily "read."

After the fabric has been prewashed, record on an index card the amount purchased, where it was bought, and the cost, as well as any specific purpose you have for it and the cleaning instructions. Also note which box it will be stored in and at what location (Fig. 4–4). Arrange this information, along with a 5″ square of the fabric, in one of the photograph album pages. Sorting these pages into color groups makes finding the right fabric easier still when you are searching for one. Eight samples per page (four on each side) can be stored in a three-ring 8½″ × 11″ binder. When the fabric has been used up and the sample is no longer necessary for the filing system, use the 5″ patches in a scrap quilt. Fabrics from clothing for each child or other family member could be made into memory quilts.

To store fabric, place it in the box indicated on the fabric index card you just made (see Fig. 4–4). Instead of piling the fabrics one on top of the other, place them on "point," side by side (Fig. 4–5). The edge of each fabric should be visible when you look down at the contents of the box. This will eliminate pulling all the fabric out of the box to find the piece you want, which is, of course, at the very bottom! If the box is full and you need to put the fabric into a different one, go back to the index card you

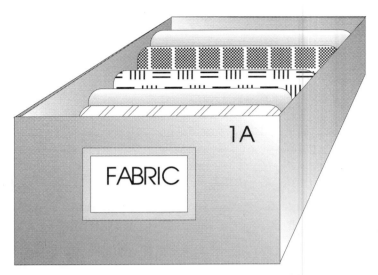

**4–5. A fabric storage box, showing fabric stored on point and box labelling.**

created for the fabric and record the change. Without much difficulty, you can now see what fabrics you have and where they are. Before you pull out the fabric, you know if you have enough for your current project and you know where to find it. You also know what store to go back to if you want to purchase more. Note: if you only use a portion of the fabric length, deduct that amount from the original total on the fabric index card, indicating how much is left.

If you're not an avid collector of fabric, you can store smaller quantities draped over hangers. Multilevel or nested skirt or pant hangers will keep fabric wrinkle-free. Several pieces can be stored together and hung on one hook. Garment or sweater bags provide convenient dust-free storage; their transparent fronts make fabric easily visible (Fig. 4–6). As this fabric supply may continue to grow, I would recommend maintaining a fabric file and noting the closet location of the fabric. If you don't feel you have enough fabric to warrant establishing a file system and have your purchasing under control, at least record the fabric details on a piece of paper and pin them in an easily found place to one corner of the fabric. Avoid storing fabric on open shelves close to fluorescent lighting or in the path of direct sunlight. Because of the constant exposure to light, faded crease marks can appear along the folds.

Any swatches that remain after you cut out larger projects can be used in quilting or appliqué projects. It's easier to store these smaller pieces together. Use dividers from liquor boxes or construct them from cardboard to divide one large box into sections (Fig. 4–7). Separate the swatches in the sections according to color. Either note on the fabric index card the amount of fabric that remains and its new location or else simply remove the card from the Fabric Filing System, as there is

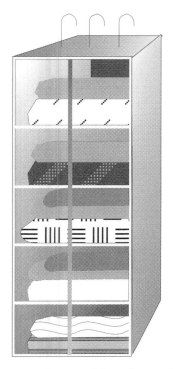

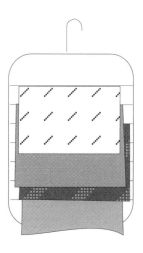

4–6. Storage ideas for small quantities of fabric. Left: garment bag; right, pants hanger.

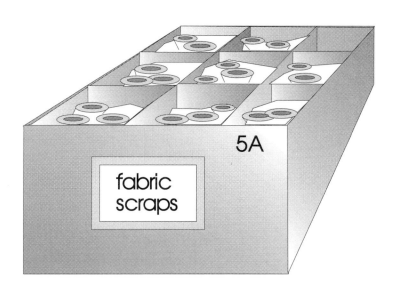

4–7. Fabric scraps are rolled up and sorted in box compartments according to color.

4–8. Patterns stored in plastic envelopes. Photo courtesy of Nancy's Notions.

insufficient fabric for any large project. Maintain your "scrap box" as a separate entity in that case.

## 4. PATTERNS

I don't know how many you have, but over the years I've collected more than 400 pants, dress, blouse, coat, maternity, children's, men's, quilt and craft patterns—practically an entire catalogue for myself! I use many patterns repeatedly; some only once in a while or once in a lifetime. If you don't feel you'll use a pattern again, the best option remains to throw it out, sell it, or give it away. However, since patterns, like clothes, come back into fashion, they're often difficult to part with. In fact, I refuse to part with any of mine. Even old and apparently outdated patterns can be useful when portions of one pattern are combined with portions of another to create individual, unique, or updated looks. I've started treating them like collector's items! No matter how many patterns you have, you can simplify their storage requirements by arranging a pattern catalogue. There are two ways to go about this.

### Method 1
Remove the pattern pieces and instructions from the pattern envelope and place them in a 8½″ × 11″ manila or plastic

**4–9. A box for storing patterns. Photo courtesy of Nancy's Notions.**

envelope (see Fig. 4–8). On the front of the envelope write the name of the pattern company and the pattern number. If you want, include a photocopy of the pattern envelope front. File the envelopes numerically by pattern number, intermingling those of different companies. For a smaller number of patterns, a pattern box can be used (Fig. 4–9). With more, consider regular-sized boxes, drawers, filing cabinets or even a pattern cabinet.

Place the empty pattern envelope in an 8½″ × 11″ photograph album page and arrange the pages numerically by pattern number in a 3-ring binder according to project category (skirts, dresses, etc.) similar to those in the original pattern catalogue (see Fig. 4–10). Patterns from all pattern companies will be intermingled. If you have so many patterns that one 3-ring binder is not going to contain them all, divide them into categories such as blouses/dresses, skirts/pants, children's/men's/ crafts, etc., and give each its own binder. Label the outside of each binder appropriately.

Slip an index card into the photograph page for each pattern, on which you have listed the details of interest about the pattern such as: *fits big/small, just love, really comfortable,* etc. Note the storage location and box number of the pattern itself. When the pattern is lent out, record the name of the borrower and the date

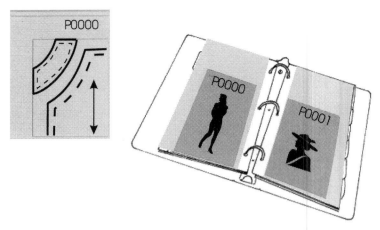

4–10. Pattern envelopes filed in an 8½″ × 11″ photograph book (right). Actual pattern pieces (left) are filed separately in a box.

borrowed. You can ask for the pattern back within a reasonable amount of time, and if you find one of the pattern pieces missing, you can inquire of the last borrower if she has seen it. Caution: be sure to check off the loan when the pattern is returned or you may end up accusing the wrong person!

## Method 2
Photocopy the front and back of each pattern envelope onto 8½″ × 11″ 3-hole paper (see Fig. 4–3, right). If you do this back to back, it'll involve a lot less paper and be easier to use than two separate sheets. In the upper right-hand corner of the sheet, note the location of the pattern. This might be a box, drawer, or file cabinet. At the bottom of the sheet, record any details of interest about the pattern. Arrange the photocopies numerically in a three-ring binder by category, similar to the pattern catalogue discussed above, with all companies' patterns intermingled. Store the actual patterns in numerical order in boxes. You'll find the pattern you need easily by going to the location listed at the top of the sheet in the 3-ring binder.

There are a couple of drawbacks to the Method 2 system. You'll only be looking at a photocopy of the design, and style details may be harder to discern than on the original. Because patterns differ in size, they won't be as easy to store as those placed in similar-sized envelopes. And, you need easy access to a photocopier. However, on the plus side, both the envelope and the pattern are stored together and the photocopied papers take up less binder space than the actual pattern envelopes will.

Your personal pattern catalogue can hold a lot more details than the original one; it will become a major reference guide for you. If you're going to ignore this advice altogether because it sounds like a lot of work, at least store patterns together by type so you don't have to go through every pattern looking for one for a dress or blouse.

## 5. INFORMATION

In addition to patterns, many of us have accumulated a wide range of other kinds of information. Books, magazines, pamphlets, and class instructions are all available to guide us in the creation of fashions, decor items, and art works. The amount of information available is phenomenal. It provides inspiration, direction, and instruction. However, more often than not, we come across a particular piece of information when it isn't required. Perversely, we may want to refer to an article we read several months or years ago to duplicate a technique in today's project. All the information sources that we gather form a personal reference library.

Probably the easiest source of information to use is a book. Although they come in various sizes, shapes and bindings, they are also the easiest to store. Because the information is contained and labelled already, the work of filing is semi-complete. This is the first source most people will refer to. The information may be contained in a pamphlet or class instruction sheet, but it's simpler to pull out a book, flip to the index and see if it contains what's needed. Therefore, books need to be kept accessible. A box will contain and store them but a shelf or out-of-the-way counter surface is much preferable.

"File" books either (1) alphabetically by author or title or (2) alphabetically by author within separate categories. The second option is probably preferable, since you can search within the desired category without going through numerous books on varying topics in an attempt to find the necessary instruction. Within such a reference library you may have categories such as tailoring, home decor, fashion tips, quilting, craft projects, and more, depending on your interests.

Keep track of the books you've purchased, not only for your inventory and personal purposes, but also so they don't become misplaced when lent out. A card can be written up for each book purchased indicating the author's name, the price, and the date purchased. Store these cards in a recipe box. Leave a space to list when the book is lent out, to whom, the person's phone number, the date it is requested back, and the date returned. When I lend a book, I ask that it be returned within two weeks. This may seem very similar to a formal library system, but after two weeks people tend to forget that they borrowed the item and therefore forget to return it. Often seeing you write down their name and phone number will be inspiration enough to get the book returned. The borrower knows you have a permanent record of her/his being there! Don't forget to record when the book is returned. Before lending any source of information, especially a book, be sure it contains your name, address and phone number. Should the borrower forget where it came from, your name inside will ensure that the book gets back home. If it's misplaced or lost, there's a lot better chance of it being returned. Labels or stamps with your name and address information can be purchased through stationery stores. (Many magazines have ads for them in the classified sections.) Not only books but invoices, receipts, and return addresses on envelopes can be stamped, which will save you from cramped hand muscles.

To keep a running total of your investment, maintain a master list with the name of the books purchased, the author, the publishing company, and the price. This is useful for insurance purposes. If you're a professional seamstress, crafter or fabric artist, many of these purchases are tax-deductible. (Be sure to keep the receipts.) A master file of this nature may be easier to maintain on a computer, since it can then be kept alphabetically. Another option is to simply list the books, as purchased, in a column and continuously add up the new total. Either way you'll know the total value of your library.

**Loose Information**

I can't resist all those freebies given out at fabric shows, stores, and demos. Pamphlets galore, all describing the latest technique for using some new wonder product, continuously collect in my bag. After each show, I dump it all out, sort it through and decide where to put these new treasures. Even though I make a point of collecting every possible piece of paper, it often seems like junk mail once I get them home. It's not, though! There's a lot of valuable information on those assorted slips of paper. The problem lies in what to do with the stuff before it becomes a junk-drawer addition and ends up in circular file "G". You can avoid purchasing a lot of expensive patterns simply by following instructions received at a demo. This is especially true in the area of home decor. Many decorative items are incredibly easy to sew. Most fabric stores have supplier-provided pamphlets in their home decor section detailing how a specific product can be used in a project. These are usually detailed enough to produce the finished product.

Traditional filing of the information by category is one way to store loose papers. A file box can be used in place of a filing cabinet if you don't have one, although a small two-drawer cabinet is a useful addition to the sewing room. If you use a cabinet, purchase a supply of hanging file folders as well as regular ones. Because hanging folders slide within the cabinet and reach from side to side, they are much neater and more contained, with little chance of information falling out and getting lost, than other folders are. Label the regular folders according to category: home decor, tailoring, quilt patterns, etc. Papers will then be filed appropriately within these folders; each can be placed within a hanging folder. Make sure duplicates of the same instructions are not being stored.

Another method for containing this information is to three-hole punch the papers and file them in a three-ring binder, which can then be shelved with your books. Simply purchase a large three-ring binder, page dividers, and some clear plastic 8″ × 10″ photograph album pages. Label the dividers accordingly and place alphabetically in the binder. Three-hole punch the information on sheets and file each behind the correct divider. Store awkward-sized papers, which are difficult to three-hole punch, in the photograph pages.

## Magazines

Most of us have favorite magazines that we read faithfully each month. Many relate directly to sewing, crafts, or quilting, but others may be more geared toward family and home life. Some of the articles may be relevant, but you won't always want to keep the whole magazine. If this is the case, tear out the article and file it with other loose paper information.

There's always the risk of storing a magazine for years and never looking at it again. We often forego looking through back issues because we would have to wade through the index of each magazine and then look up the page to find out if the information is what we want. Some magazines provide an index of articles published in the previous year. This can be filed with the issues it pertains to, which makes finding a specific article easier. Unfortunately, most magazines don't provide an overall summary; however, by photocopying the contents page of each magazine and filing this collective "index" with the issues, you can provide one for yourself.

You will probably want to store most magazines by date, with the current issue either first or last. Store the issues on a shelf, in a magazine box (Fig. 4–11), or with magazine clips in a three-ring binder. I prefer the last two alternatives, because they allow for easy movement of the magazines while keeping them together as a unit. Label the box or binder with the name of the magazine and the "to" and "from" dates of the issues.

If you really want to know what you have and where it is, start an index of all the articles. Again dividing the articles by subject category, keep a continuous reference of what information you have by writing (or typing) the name of the article, what it pertains to, and where it can be found. (A computer would be a definite asset for such an endeavor.) If you require any

4–11. Magazines, stored in a magazine box.

information on a specific subject, it can be located easily by referring to the reference manual you have created. This involves a lot of work! Personally, I'm not that dedicated. Unless you use magazine articles repeatedly, it's not worth the effort involved. In most cases, being able to refer to the collective index of photocopied pages is adequate.

There's no use storing information you don't need. It simply takes up space and collects dust while others may be able to make use of it. Donate any back issues that you never look at to the local library, a home economics class or guild, and sewing club libraries.

Magazines are as valuable as books and equally expensive. As with your books, you should keep an index card to note when an issue is borrowed. You also may want a master list for inventory and insurance purposes.

## 6. NOTIONS

Probably the hardest supplies to store are notions, because they come in so many shapes and sizes. Threads, zippers, buttons, elastic, laces, trims and bindings all need to be stored efficiently. Let me reemphasize the necessity for same-sized storage units. This is critical when storing notions. There can be many, many containers of individual items. While the items may differ in size, same-sized containers will stack properly with little lost storage space. Odd-sized containers create "dead" space between them.

You may find yourself ducking as they tumble onto the floor in front of you.

Storing individual notions by color allows you to obtain the most suitable choice in the quickest manner possible without having to sort through each item. If you have drawer space available, drawer dividers or cutlery trays are useful for breaking them up. Stationery and department stores are wonderful resource places. Boxes for fly fishing ties or nuts and bolts are also ideal storage units. You'll be amazed at what's there and will find some perfect storage units for sewing supplies if you take the time to look. Before heading to the store have a clear idea of what supplies require storage, and avoid buying unnecessary or incorrectly sized units.

Another solution is the taboret, a popular item with commercial artists also. Figure 4–12 shows two models of such storage units. Both are wonderful storage units for notions. Equipped with casters, they can be pulled near the cutting, construction, pressing or fitting area as needed, and then stored in place when not in use.

If you've purchased notions to coordinate with a specific fabric, note on the fabric index card that these notions exist and where they are stored. This eliminates duplicate purchases or additional trips to the storage area to gather up the supplies for the current project. In addition, you may want to mark the notion for the

4–12. Two sizes of taboret, useful for storing notions. Photo courtesy of Ideal Creations.

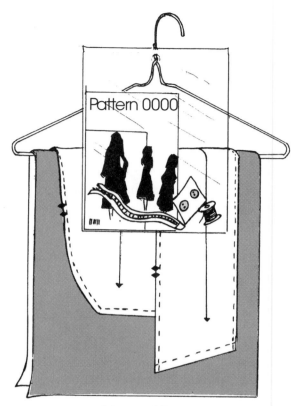

**4–13. You could store fabric, notions, and the pattern for a project together on a hanger.**

specific project so you don't use it for another purpose. All notions purchased for a specific project could be stored together with the fabric. Drape the fabric over a hanger. Place the notions in a plastic bag, and slip the bag over the top of the hanger. If you have a specific pattern in mind, place it in the bag also, which keeps the entire project together (Fig. 4–13).

Many sewers prefer to keep the pieces of one project together. However, I prefer to keep mine separate since, occasionally, I change the original use of the pieces. If I have purchased fabric for a blouse with coordinating buttons and accessories and then decide to use that fabric in a quilt project, the notions become redundant. By having them in a separate area, they are visible and can be used in other projects. If you have them all together and you change your mind about the fabric's purpose, you simply put the notions and pattern back into storage and carry on.

*Thread.* Tangled threads can lead to hours of frustration. For the longest time I kept mine in a plastic box. I'd roll up the strands and chuck 'em in there. Occasionally I managed to clip in the thread or even tape it in place, hoping to avoid tangles, but more often than not I simply threw them in. The result was a mass of intertangled threads, pretty to look at colorwise, but very discouraging to separate. To make matters worse, I'd often slipped a needle into the thread rounds after hand sewing and hadn't removed it, so things could get a little prickly. Thread racks are available in all sizes and shapes to save you from this headache (Fig. 4–14). You can buy them for both regular and serger-size spools. Usually they're wall-mounted, as this creates less clutter on the counter, although some racks will stand and can be placed on a counter near the construction area. Some racks are decorative; others are purely functional. If you have the wall or

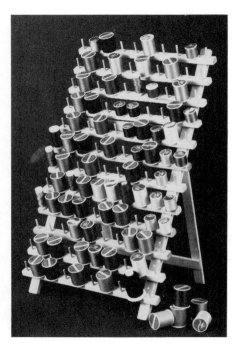
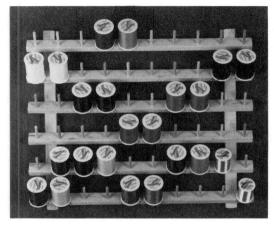

4–14. Several styles of thread rack. Photo courtesy of June Tailor, Inc.

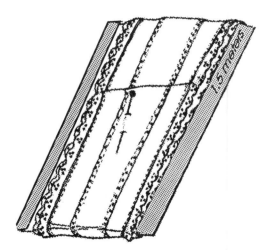

**4–15. Lace or trim can be wrapped around a cardboard core.**

counter space, having thread visible and accessible is the best option.

There are several options besides spool racks. A thread board can be made from a piece of plywood and finishing nails. Paint the wood to coordinate with the sewing room, hammer in evenly spaced nails, and hang up the thread supplies on the nails. Clear plastic storage containers, preferably with dividers, can be purchased to keep thread neat. With these containers you can see the contents without opening every box, and the lid keeps them from spilling. Learn from my example and keep those thread ends tucked in! If you don't have the wall or counter space available or don't want thread visible, empty envelope boxes also work well to store thread. Dividers can be made to separate the individual colors.

Whenever possible, store wound bobbins with the thread spool they were wound from. You can purchase a device to hold the bobbin and spool together, like Handi-Bobs. They fit most bobbin and thread spools available on the market. Otherwise, a bobbin box stores up to 21 bobbins neatly. If they are kept in the same area as the thread, the bobbins are equally accessible. If you're using pegboard, a thread board, or a thread rack, simply store the bobbin on the same peg as the matching thread.

*Laces, Trims, and Bindings.* If you have the drawer space, trims and laces can be stored there, or perhaps in a wicker basket, gift bag, envelope box, or small garbage can. Whichever you choose, wrap pieces of lace, trim, or binding around cardboard cores from wrapping paper, ribbon, or other paper products and secure the ends with a pin or piece of tape to prevent unravelling (Fig. 4–15). Record the amount of trim, the cost, the place purchased, and any other information you might need on the cardboard core or on a piece of paper tucked into a fold of the trim. The entire length shouldn't have to be unravelled to find out how much is there.

*Buttons.* Everyone has had a project where one or two buttons are left over. What do you do with them? One additional button could be stitched inconspicuously to the wrong side of the garment. When a button is lost from the outside, this one replaces it. Odd buttons can be stored in decorative boxes, baby food jars, or similar-sized containers. You could also place the buttons in small resealable plastic bags and hang them by color on a pegboard. These buttons can often be used in craft projects or on children's clothing. The trend in the fashion industry lately has been to use a variety of buttons on shirt or skirt fronts. This certainly is one way to use up odds and ends.

Buttons are a fashion accessory and many are extremely expensive. To be unable to locate them and have to repurchase is a waste of time and money. You may be unable to purchase the original choice again, and if you settle for second best, you then face the dilemma of whether or not you're going to undo the work and sew on your first-choice buttons when you finally locate them.

Store buttons together. On several occasions I've purchased buttons specifically for a project, put them somewhere, and then couldn't find them later. I've then gone back to the store and bought some more. Invariably, within a couple of weeks, the original batch would show up. Since then I've learned to store buttons in a "safe" place. If you've purchased them to coordinate with a specific fabric, store them together or note the purpose on the button card. Join more than one card of buttons with an elastic band. Snaps and other fasteners can be stored in the same way as buttons. Any tools necessary for securing the fastenings should be kept at the same location.

*Zippers.* The easiest way to sort zippers is by hanging them up on pegboard, using the cardboard sizing label at the top. Arrange them so that the color and length can be quickly noted. A strip of magnetic tape on a piece of 1″ × 1″ wood or pegboard can be used (Fig. 4–16, left). Or, sort zippers according to color and length along a hanger, using the cardboard sizing labels to hold them on. Consider clipping them together with a large metal clip or clothespin (Fig. 4–16, right). Then thread a cord through the top, tie a knot and hang them on a hook. For a designer touch, tole paint the clothespins!

Keep groups of similar-sized zippers together. You probably won't have a large stock of zippers, so separation by color probably isn't necessary. If you do, clip zippers of one color together with the shortest in front and longest to the back. Or, if you'd prefer to avoid hanging them up altogether, roll the zippers with the sizing labels to the outside and store in a drawer or divided box.

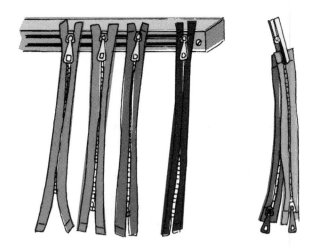

**4–16. Two ways of hanging zippers. Left: magnetic strip. Right: clothespin.**

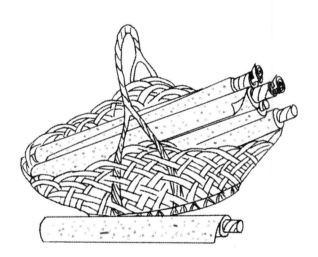

**4–17. Interfacings can be rolled on cardboard rolls and stored in a basket.**

*Interfacing.* Interfacings, especially fusible ones, should be kept wrinkle-free. Fold and stack interfacings neatly in a drawer or on a shelf. You also could hang them on a hanger or drape them over a towel rack, or roll them onto empty paper-towel rolls, secure them with an elastic band, and store them in a wicker basket near the cutting surface (Fig. 4–17).

If you use a variety of different interfacings, be sure to keep a copy of the instructions together with each interfacing. Each has been developed for a specific purpose, and you'll want to use the one most suitable for your project. If you find you like the effect of one type, you'll need this information to purchase it again.

*Elastic.* Elastic appears to be a pretty basic subject, but there are so many varieties on the market that choosing the right one can be difficult. Woven, ribbed, braided, cycling, see-through, sport, clear, drawcord, swimsuit, lingerie, flat no-roll, and elastic thread are all available, in addition to the basic ½″, ¾″, 1″, etc. Do you need all of these? Probably not, but you will need an assortment of different widths. Although I don't utilize this notion frequently, when I use elastic I usually only need a portion of the length purchased. I keep the packaging and roll and carefully tuck the unused portion back in. This keeps the elastics from getting tangled. Sort the elastic into groupings according to size, and store them in a divided container, with each size and type separate (Fig. 4–18). You should be able to open the storage unit and choose the correct size immediately, without having to pick around and sort through them all.

*Needlework Supplies.* Embroidery or cross-stitch is often used to embellish a fashion garment or accent children's clothing. Quilters may use embroidery floss or yarns for decorative stitches. Needlework involves canvas, needles, embroidery floss or yarn, hoops, stretcher bars, and instructions. Because needlework is a "take-along" art form, you'll want to keep supplies together and easily movable. Additional supplies that are not in use at the time can be stored in . . . yes, you guessed it . . . a box! Properly labelled of course!

If you do a lot of needlework and want your hoops, stretcher bars, and fabrics to be more accessible, hang the hoops and bars on a pegboard with other supplies. Needlework fabrics can be arranged in the same manner as the fashion or quilting fabrics. The sample of fabric can be much smaller than the previously

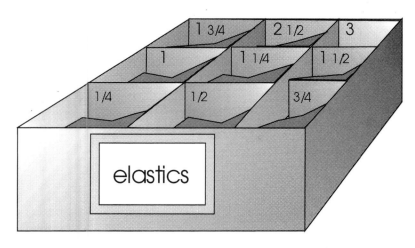

**4–18. A box for storing elastics, by width.**

mentioned 5″ fabric squares for sewing. A 1″ to 2″ square will provide a good idea of the overall look. On an index card, list the name of the fabric, its hole count, weave information or content, where purchased, the yardage amount, and the fabric's storage location. Also note on the card whether you've purchased this cloth for a specific project, and what book the needlework chart is located in.

I've done a considerable amount of cross-stitch and have found the following format for storing embroidery flosses works well. This technique has been shown in my classes, and the majority of students have adopted it. I use baby bottle liners and cut off the serrated fold-down tops. (There are also resealable plastic bags available at most needlework shops.) Each embroidery floss is cut into 36″ lengths, folded and placed in a bottle liner. A small label in the upper right hand corner contains the color code. The plastic pouches are then numerically filed in a picnic basket (Fig. 4–19). Yes, that was correct, a picnic basket! I put a small box in one corner to contain embroidery scissors, spare needles, a pad of paper and pencil, the manufacturer's embroidery floss checklist, and additional plastic pouches. There is room on top of the floss to lay my chart, fabric, and embroidery hoop. When I want to go somewhere, I just pick up my basket and go! Everything I could need is already there.

Use magazine boxes or a 3-ring binder with transparent acetate photo album pages and magazine clips to keep patterns and

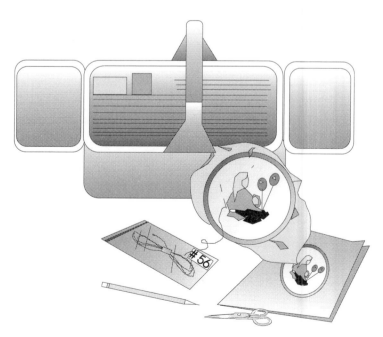

4–19. With its easy portability, a picnic basket is ideal for storing needlework supplies.

instructions in order. It's not advisable to three-hole punch needlework patterns, as you may lose portions of the chart.

## 7. FINAL NOTE

As I stated earlier, there are an infinite number of supplies that you will need to store. One of the obvious ones I haven't mentioned is the wide variety of hand sewing and sewing machine needles available. Using the above system you can incorporate any additional products in a workable manner, however.

Any specialty area you are involved with may require specific considerations. Take quilting, for example—my specialty interest. It has its own set of supplies: template materials, designer rulers, paper patchwork squares, freezer paper, rotary blades, specialty needles, thimbles, design paper, marking pens, thread, etc. As much as possible, I incorporate these supplies into existing storage areas. Rulers are hung at the cutting surface, thread on the spool racks, needles kept with other needles, fabric sorted into my Fabric Filing System, etc., with the remainder of supplies are kept in labelled boxes . . . of course!

From reading the above chapter, you'll have realized quite quickly that I believe in storage boxes. I have a large closet in my sewing room where I store the various boxes of fabrics, yarns, cross-stitch supplies, and craft items. I label each box. If they contain fabric or patterns, I cross-reference those boxes to my Personal Pattern Catalogue or my Fabric Filing System. If the box contains something out of the ordinary, such as supplies for dried flower arrangements, I list the contents on one side of the index card in the plastic envelope outside the box. On the other side of the card, in large letters, I write Dried Flower Arrangements. This side of the index card is placed face out. At a glance I know that if I'm making a dried flower arrangement, what I want is probably in that box. I can read the list on the reverse side just to be sure before digging through the box. Needless to say, when you're finished with supplies, it's a good idea to put them back in the same box they came from.

I also think pegboard is the greatest solution for notions. It keeps them both neat and visible. If it's impossible to hang the actual notion, resealable plastic bags can be used. These can be purchased in large quantities from a dry goods supplier with hang holes already punched.

Is this system complicated? Not really! It does require time to set up but you'll be rewarded by an organized working environment. You'll also save money as you will be using up supplies you already have instead of constantly buying additional ones because you can't find the old ones. Best of all, frustration levels will be at a minimum and creative ones at a high.

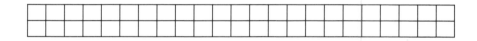

# · 5 ·

# Project Organization

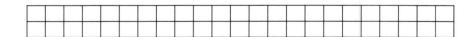

When I build a puzzle, I separate all the pieces at the beginning. I remove those with straight edges for building the frame. Different colors are placed in separate groupings. "Special" pieces are carefully put aside to become the focal point. Then, I systematically begin putting the pieces back together again. First I build the frame, fill in the sky, fill in the foreground and the background. Then, I take those special pieces and shape the focal point. In the end, I have completed the picture. I've used a tried and true system. I haven't been frustrated, but neither have I been bored. I've enjoyed the creative process.

Completing a sewing project is like building a puzzle. The original product is cut into various odd-shaped pieces that are twisted and turned until they fit back together. The puzzle simply becomes the picture once more, but the fabric can become three-dimensional, taking on a shape, form, and life of its own. Each project is an artistic endeavor.

Whether you're sewing a one-of-a-kind designer suit, an intricate quilt pattern, or that old favorite shirt for the twentieth time, each project will go through a series of steps from beginning to end. In many cases the order of those steps can be altered from the original pattern instructions and the project organized in a faster, more efficient manner. Being fast and efficient doesn't mean sewing becomes boring, repetitive, or strictly functional. On the contrary, by doing similar functions together, you'll have additional time for new techniques and for being more creative, or you'll simply produce more projects in the same amount of time.

There are infinite possibilities as to what can be produced in your sewing room; however, I'll concentrate on fashion sewing and quilting projects as these are the two more common or popular areas of sewing. Because the approach to each is slightly different, they'll be dealt with individually.

# Sewing Fashions

A long time ago, way back when, just about everyone sewed their own clothing, or at least the women sewed for their families. There was no other choice. A noted few were able to afford a seamstress or tailor to personally customize their clothing, but the majority of the population created their own. As time moved on, ready-made clothes became available in various price ranges to the point where very few people sewed their own and an even smaller elite had personal designers. In fact, at one point sewing your own clothing simply was not done!

Now fashion sewing is returning to vogue. With the high cost of quality clothing and the generally poor quality of affordable clothing, we're once again interested in creating our own fashions. That way we get the style, color, fit, and design we want, all tailored to our specific requirements. We can avoid the faddish styles, inappropriate to our figure type or age, which tend to dominate the market every season. Plus, we get the hours of enjoyment and creativity that go into producing fashions not only for ourselves but for our family and home. There's a great deal of satisfaction in creating it all by yourself.

However, with the time constraints many of us are working under—juggling work, family, home and special interests—the need to organize each project is paramount. The earlier chapters in the book discussed the organization of space and supplies. When constructing a fashion garment, you also need to organize the project and your supplies. Each project can be broken down into units, such as cutting and sewing, which are completable in time frames ranging from 10 to 30 minutes. Awareness of these units will allow you to get organized and to accomplish much more in less time.

## 1. ORGANIZING PROJECT SUPPLIES

Your overall enjoyment of a project and the time and money savings to you depend on how well you organize project supplies. Unless everything is assembled at the beginning, production will be "stop and go." Leaving the room or running to the store wastes valuable sewing time; also, you'll probably pick up extra articles when you run out to shop that you hadn't planned on buying, thereby adding to your expenses. Before beginning a project, purchase and collect all the necessary parts for constructing the whole. Read the back of the fashion pattern envelope. It provides information on the fabric and notions required. Think of these as the ingredients. Without the fabric, interfacing, lining, shoulder pads, thread, fasteners, etc. (everything needed to finish the project) you can't bake the "cake."

Once you've purchased everything and are ready to start, break down the package. Move the pattern, fabric, interfacing and lining to the cutting surface; move the notions—such as thread, zippers, and buttons—to the construction surface. Any fitting aids, such as shoulder pads, will be placed near the fitting area or mirror, or kept with the other notions. Don't stack supplies in an area where they won't be used; this causes congestion and frustration. You'll find yourself constantly picking up the same item and moving it out of the way.

You may find it easier to keep a checklist for each project to help you maintain your overall perspective and provide a reference for any supplies that need to be purchased. I've included one for your use, the Project Supplies Organization Checklist on page 93. Feel free to photocopy it. When a project is complete, file the checklist with the pattern or in the Pattern Filing System (see Chapter 4). If you used any unfamiliar interfacing, lining fabric, or notions, note your opinion of these supplies on the checklist for future projects, as well as any comments on the success of the fashion.

Keep a shopping list. As supplies become diminished, list what you need. When a sale is on, simply grab the list and stock up at the lower costs. Many times I've arrived at a sale thinking I knew exactly what I need, only to be bombarded by all those good prices and forget what I originally went for. A list helps! One of the stores near where I live has an early-bird sale several times a year. You get up extremely early, arriving at the store before the sun even comes up to take advantage of 40% savings. The only problem is you're still half asleep and not thinking too well. After I'd been to several of these sales and bought fabric for quilts but forgot batting and thread, which should have been pretty obvious, I learned the value of a shopping list.

## 2. PRETREATING FABRIC

If you've just purchased the fabric for the project or if you don't pretreat stored fabrics, pretreat the fabric before cutting the garment out. The fibre content and fabric care instructions found on the bolt end will dictate the prewash method. If you've had the fabric for a while, this information should be noted in your Fabric Filing System. It is usually advisable to pretreat the fabric using the method by which the finished garment will be cleaned. There's a finish adhered to the fabric at the mill to prevent it from soiling or wrinkling during shipping, which is removed during the pretreating process. If it isn't removed, stitching can appear unbalanced or skip. Pretreating also preshrinks the fabric. After spending considerable time constructing a garment, you don't want it to shrink out of proportion during the first washing. This is costly both in time and money.

## 3. ASSEMBLING THE PATTERN PIECES

Pin up the sewing instructions and the pattern envelope near your cutting surface. Circle the layout and pattern pieces required for the view you're making, or highlight them with a marker to make the information more visible and easier to see at a glance.

Separate and press the tissue pieces needed, using a dry iron; steam can ripple and distort them. Refold any unnecessary pieces and replace in the pattern envelope. Lay the pressed pieces on a flat surface until they are needed, or drape them over a chair or hanger to avoid rewrinkling them. Unnecessary and repetitive procedures are no fun; you don't want to re-press.

## 4. PATTERN ALTERATIONS

Few of us have a perfect body that matches up to the pattern company's measurements. Unless you do, you'll need to alter the pattern to your proportions. You will find that the pattern alterations you need are often similar from pattern to pattern. After you become familiar with the fit of patterns from each company, you'll find that you make the same basic alterations to each pattern from that company without much difficulty. When you've completed the alterations, remember to note the changes on an index card, and staple it to the pattern instructions for future reference.

Have a friend accurately take your measurements. If you prefer to keep these private, hire a professional seamstress. There are a variety of measurements beyond the basic bust, waist and hip measurements that will make fitting and altering patterns easier and the look of the finished garment much more professional. The Sewing Measurements Chart on page 86, provided by Butterick Company, Ltd., explains how to take those measurements, which are illustrated in Fig. 5–1. When they are complete, tack the measurements where they'll be readily available, along with those of family members or anyone else you sew for. Books on tailoring will provide information on how to go about altering a pattern. A professional seamstress may give you lessons for a nominal fee; fabric stores sometimes provide classes on this subject. Many figure faults can be successfully hidden once you know what to do.

## 5. CUTTING OUT THE PATTERN

Now that the fabric's chosen and pretreated, the pattern pieces separated, and any necessary alterations made, you're ready to cut out the pieces. This requires a significant amount of time and of

# SEWING MEASUREMENTS CHART

## Circumference Measurements

\_\_\_\_ **Bust:** Measure around the fullest part with tape straight across your back (1).
\_\_\_\_ **Chest:** Measure around body at underarm above breasts (2).
\_\_\_\_ **Diaphragm:** Measure around rib cage, halfway between bust and waist (3).
\_\_\_\_ **Waist:** Measure at waist (4).
\_\_\_\_ **Hip:** Mark tape positions with pins on leotard and measure from waist to pins to establish the next three hip positions.
\_\_\_\_ **High Hip:** Measure around 2"–4" below waist over top of hip bones (5).
\_\_\_\_ **Full Hip:** Measure around fullest part, usually 7"–9" from waist (6).
\_\_\_\_ **Thigh Bulge:** With feet together, measure around both legs at fullest point of upper thigh (7).
\_\_\_\_ **Leg:** Measure leg at fullest part of thigh (8),
\_\_\_\_ knee (9),
\_\_\_\_ calf (10),
\_\_\_\_ and instep (11).
\_\_\_\_ **Neck:** Measure circumference at the fullest part (12).
\_\_\_\_ **Biceps:** Measure circumference at the fullest part (13).
\_\_\_\_ **Wrist:** Measure at wrist bone (14).

## Length Measurements

\_\_\_\_ **Front Neck to Waist:** Measure from the base of your neck (the hollow between collarbones) to your waist at center front (15).
**Front Length:** Measure from the prominent:
\_\_\_\_ back neck bone over your shoulder to your bust point (16),
\_\_\_\_ and from bust point to center front at waist (17).
\_\_\_\_ **Shoulder:** Measure along shoulder from the base of the neck to your shoulder bone (18).
**Arm Length:** With your arm slightly bent, measure:
\_\_\_\_ from your shoulder bone to your elbow (19),
\_\_\_\_ and to your wrist above your little finger (20).
\_\_\_\_ Total of both measurements
\_\_\_\_ **Back Length:** Measure from prominent neck bone at center back to waist (21).
\_\_\_\_ **Back Width:** Measure across the back, with arms moderately forward, from the crease where arm meets the body to the opposite crease (22).
\_\_\_\_ **Hip Length:** Distance between waist and full hip at side (23).
\_\_\_\_ **Crotch Depth:** Sit on a hard, straight-backed chair; using a ruler, measure at side from waist to chair seat (24).
\_\_\_\_ **Crotch Length:** Measure between legs from center front waist to center back waist (not shown).
\_\_\_\_ **Pants Length:** Measure at side from waist to floor, or to desired length (25).
\_\_\_\_ **Skirt Length:** Measure from center back waist to desired hemline (26).

course accuracy, but there are several ways to shorten the time involved.

Cut two layers together whenever possible. For example, if you're making a lined dress, lay the lining fabric over the fashion fabric and cut the two together (Fig. 5–2). However, avoid this if the fashion fabric requires matching, such as plaids or stripes, or if it's too bulky, as it can create more problems than it's worth. Also, the two fabrics should be the same width.

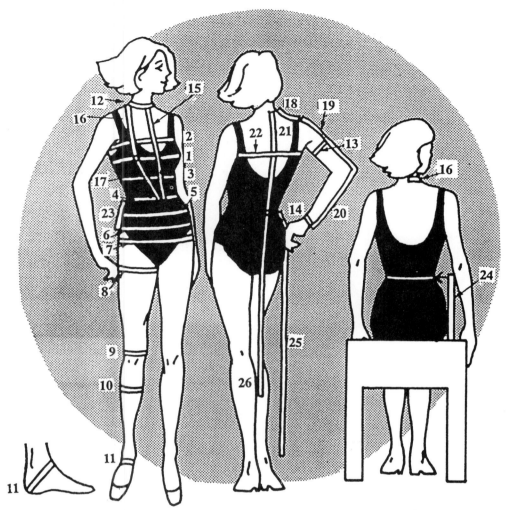

**5–1. Diagrams for sewing measurements. Courtesy of Butterick Company, Ltd.**

There are two products to consider if you do a lot of cutting out that will help relieve the stress, cramping and pain that can come from continual cutting. The first is a pair of therapeutic craft gloves, such as those manufactured by Handeze. These are 4-way stretch gloves that provide nonrestrictive support for hands and wrists. The second is an easy-to-use scissors such as Fiskars Soft-touch scissors (Fig. 5–3).

Instead of pinning the pattern pieces in place, use fabric weights (I've substituted tin cans on occasion! Small ones, like tuna or salmon cans work very well.) You can purchase decorative weights or smaller disks and bars (Fig. 5–4 and 5–5). Secure the pattern pieces along the grainline with pins, but use weights to keep the edges secure. Weight the edge along which you're cutting; shift the weights around as you work, but be careful that

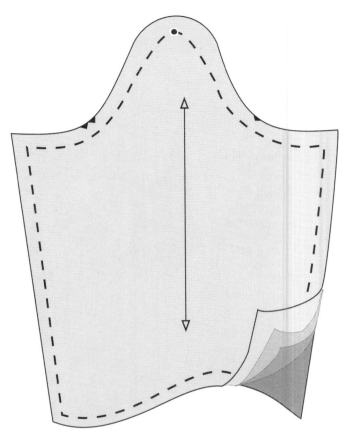

5–2. If possible, cut several layers of fabric together to save time.

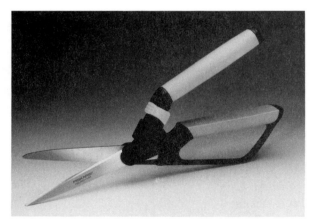

5–3. An easy-to-use scissors, like this Fiskars Soft-Touch scissors, is an aid if you will be doing a great deal of cutting. Photo courtesy of Fiskars, Inc.

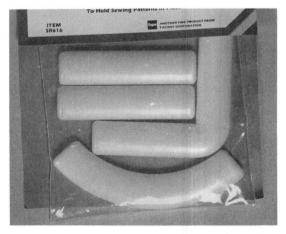

5–4. A set of weights. Photo courtesy of Tacony Corporation.

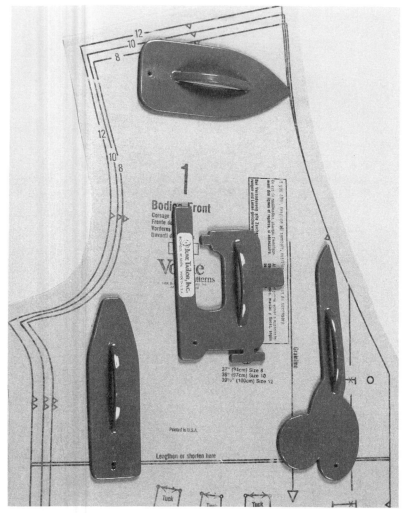

**5–5. Weights like these decorative ones can take the place of pinning and save time. Photo courtesy of June Tailor, Inc.**

the pattern remains flat against the fabric. As you cut, don't worry about notches or markings. Simply cut straight along the cutting line. I'll describe in the next unit how to do the markings.

Two pattern pieces that contain straight cutting lines can be butted against each other. Instead of cutting one line at a time, you'll be cutting two at once (Fig. 5–6). Avoid stretching or adjusting one pattern piece to meet the other, as this may result in cutting the fabric off grain. Rather, match along the straight line as much as possible, and cut the unmatched lengths separately.

Rotary cutters can be used to cut out garments. Attachments are available to add the seam allowance as you cut. This is especially great with patterns that don't include the seam allowance. When cutting along straight edges, use a ruler to make

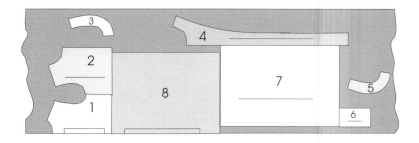

**5–6. Butting pattern pieces with straight lines together means you only have to make one cut instead of two. Note how pieces 1, 2, 6, 7, and 8 all butt against each other.**

**5–7. A wave blade (right) and pinking blade (left) for a rotary cutter. Photo courtesy of Fiskars, Inc.**

one long, clean cut. If you're not using a rotary cutter, 8″ shears work best, but should be very sharp. Clean edges make seams neater and easier to stitch. Your fabric shears shouldn't be used for cutting anything other than fabric.

Fiskars produces two specialty blades that can be used with their rotary cutter. One is a pinking blade and the other is a wave blade (Fig. 5–7). Besides the obvious application for reducing ravelling and completing a pinked seam finish while cutting out the garment, both blades are extremely useful for crafts, sewing, quilting, and other projects.

When you're making more than one project from the same pattern at one time, stack the fabrics with the most slippery on

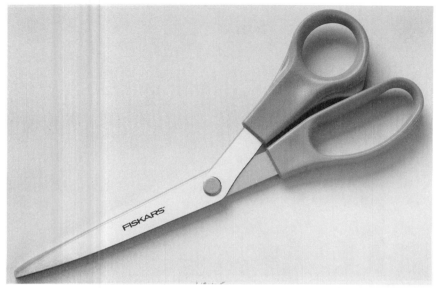

**5–8. A scissors with a 45° edge is used for cutting several layers at once. Photo courtesy of Fiskars, Inc.**

top, and cut them out together. This won't work if one of the fabrics has a design to match, is too bulky, or is a different width than the other. If you're not using a rotary cutter to cut these multiple layers, your scissors should be very sharp. Fiskars has designed an 8″ multi-layer scissors with a special 45° edge for this purpose (Fig. 5–8).

Anytime you're cutting and sewing multiples, try to coordinate the fabrics so that the same thread color can be used to stitch more than one. Avoid changing thread for each project, and sew them all at once. Not having to thread and rethread the machine continuously is a great time-saver. When one color is not suitable for all fabrics, choose one that will blend with the majority of colors.

## 6. MARKING

Marking can be accomplished quite quickly and, since it makes construction so much easier, you don't want to avoid the marking step.

Pressure-sensitive symbols like Pattern Pals are one of the newest concepts in pattern marking. These symbols can be pressed in place, marking the location of small and large dots, notches, darts, or tucks (Fig. 5–9). Just about any pattern marking can be transferred to the fabric with this tool. These are great for use on leather, suede or other difficult to mark fabrics, or on busy prints. Heirloom sewers use them because they leave

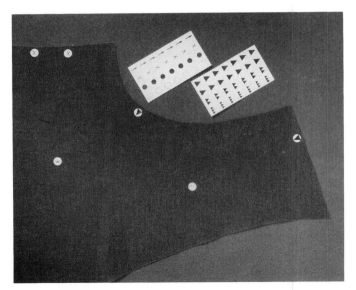

**5–9. Pressure-sensitive symbols speed transfer of pattern markings. Photo courtesy of Nancy's Notions, Inc.**

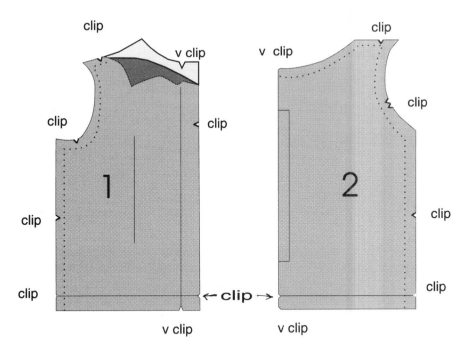

**5–10. Small clips in seam allowances can serve to mark dots or notches.**

no residue and are highly visible while they are in place.

A series of small clips into the seam allowance also can serve as markers (Fig. 5–10). Keep the clips to a short ¼″ in case the

## PROJECT SUPPLIES ORGANIZATION CHECKLIST

Pattern: _____

Fabric Requirements: _____

Interfacing: _____

Lining: _____

**Notions:**

| | |
|---|---|
| Thread | _____ |
| Buttons | _____ |
| Zipper | _____ |
| Elastic | _____ |
| Shoulder pads | _____ |
| Snaps | _____ |
| Hook and eyes | _____ |
| Twill tape | _____ |
| Seam binding | _____ |
| Other | _____ |
| | _____ |
| | _____ |

Fabric Swatch:

Fabric Content: _____

Fabric Care: _____

Comments:
_____
_____
_____
_____

seamline needs to be adjusted later and to prevent weakened seams. Use a straight clip to mark notches and to indicate the end of dart legs and hemlines. Use V clips for center back and front on the main pattern pieces, collars, and facings.

If you want a clearer mark, but find tailor tacks tedious, washable markers or a #4H lead pencil can be used to indicate circles. Always mark the wrong side of the fabric on the seam line or slightly within the seam allowance. To avoid permanent markings, pretest markers on a scrap of fabric prior to using them, and be sure they wash out.

Several methods can be used to indicate right and wrong fabric sides, such as a piece of masking tape, weaving a pin through the center of the fabric piece with the pin's head on the right side, or pencilling a small R within the seam allowance at the top of each piece on the right side. Whatever method used, be sure markings are transferred to all layers cut. This includes multiple garments, if you are cutting them to together, as well as the lining fabric or interfacing.

## 7. INTERFACING

Tests aren't time-savers, or are they? In the long run they can prevent costly mistakes. It only takes a few seconds to do a test swatch and make sure that the interfacing and fashion fabric are compatible. Recutting the collar or front facing is time-consuming and costly if you end up having to purchase additional fabric or can no longer complete the garment. This is especially important when you're using an interfacing for the first time as its suitability to the fabric is not guaranteed.

Make an interfacing pattern by laying wax paper over the pattern piece and tracing ⅛″ away from the stitching line, within the seam allowance, extending the line to the outer edge where necessary (Fig. 5–11). Making a pattern for the interfacing may sound like a waste, but it can actually save you time and money. It prevents your needing to use the pattern piece to cut out an interfacing piece larger than necessary and then pare it down to the correct size, throwing away the excess in the process.

Use fusible interfacing whenever possible. They are suitable for 98% of all fabrics and add the shape and stability garments

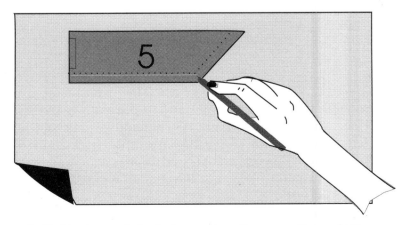

5–11. **Tracing an interfacing pattern from a pattern piece.**

require with a minimum amount of effort. Since the application method can differ for different fusible interfacings, ask for a set of instructions when purchasing the product. When applying interfacing, fuse it to all relevant fabric pieces at the same time instead of doing each piece as it's required.

## 8. GARMENT CONSTRUCTION

The speed and ability with which you construct a garment is directly related to your level of experience. After sewing for years, many seamstresses don't even read the instruction sheet. For a beginner this may sound unbelievable. But, after completing several similar projects, the beginner also will start to anticipate the next steps, and soon she or he too will be completing the construction independently.

There are several methods that can be utilized for garment construction. The first one I refer to as the beginner method, although anyone can benefit from these tips. Two others are the assembly line method and the flat construction method. Each of these results in a finished garment; they just use different routes to get there.

### The Beginner Method

Most beginners want to follow the step-by-step procedures exactly as they are written on the pattern instruction sheet until they're more familiar with the steps involved. This makes sense since if you don't know what's happening, you won't know where to make changes. The pattern instruction sheet usually has broken the garment down into construction units. An example of these units for a blouse, as shown in Fig. 5–12, would be:

1. Front and back
2. Collar
3. Neckline and front facings
4. Sleeves and underarm seams
5. Plackets and/or cuffs
6. Finishing.

After cutting out the pattern, group the fabric pieces into the same construction units as the pattern instructions divides them, and stack them in order of use. This eliminates your constantly sorting through the pile of pieces searching for the desired piece; it also will help you to determine if you've cut out everything. Small pattern pieces, such as facings, can easily be missed during the pattern layout and cutting stage. (Sometimes even bigger

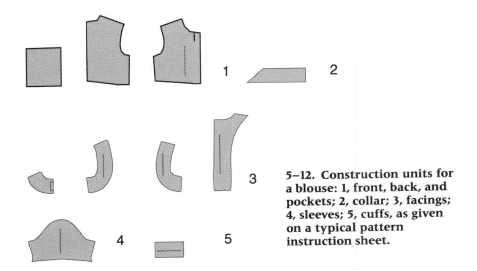

**5–12.** Construction units for a blouse: 1, front, back, and pockets; 2, collar; 3, facings; 4, sleeves; 5, cuffs, as given on a typical pattern instruction sheet.

pieces can be overlooked. The other day I cut out a blouse and totally forgot about the sleeves until this stage!) Remove all pins except those securing the pattern to the fabric at the grainline.

Begin stitching the units together, following the pattern instructions. Read the instructions for each unit thoroughly before proceeding. Give yourself plenty of time to complete the unit you've begun. Sew slowly and steadily. Accuracy is more important than speed. As a beginner, I assumed that the faster I sewed, the sooner I'd get onto the next project and in no time at all I'd have a wonderful designer wardrobe. Not true! When I learned to sew at a steady, more moderate speed and take care matching seam allowances and markings, I made fewer mistakes and completed garments that had a more professional look. My speed increased with practice.

Never leave a mistake uncorrected. Remove the stitches and ready the garment for restitching before putting the project down. Most mistakes don't require much time to remove and you'll have a more positive outlook coming back to your sewing if you don't have to rip stitches before continuing with the project.

If you become frustrated with a project, leave it for a while and return when you're in a better frame of mind. Often you can solve the problem by distancing yourself from it. When errors stare us in the face and we don't know what to do, we can become so tied up in the problem that the solution isn't obvious. Distance will give you a clearer perspective. When you're so frustrated you want to roll the fabric up in a little ball and aim it at the nearest garbage can, don't give up. Seek the advice of friends or another seamstress. Sewers love to share what they know with other sewers. Most fabric stores have talented sales people who are willing to help out. There are a wide range of books on basic and advanced sewing techniques that are excellent reference material.

Classes are usually available for all levels of expertise. And, if you'd like to take a class at home, rent or buy a video for on-the-spot training, right in your own living room!

## The Assembly-Line Method

Using the assembly-line method, the steps for garment construction are arranged so similar activities, such as stitching and pressing, are completed in groupings throughout the garment's construction, which in turn saves a lot of movement around the sewing center. You're not sewing a seam, pressing it, sewing another, and pressing it repetitively. Since your movements are more coordinated and controlled, you can save a lot of time and energy.

Summarizing units 1 through 7 described earlier in this chapter, the pattern pieces already have been sorted, the tissue patterns have been pressed, and the fabric has been cut out. The fashion fabric, lining, and interfacing all have been marked, and the interfacing has been fused in place. Now we're ready to stitch the seams together. Before stitching, prefinish the seam allowances. Work around each fabric piece, finishing the seam allowances that will be exposed to friction. You won't need to finish unexposed areas such as yoke or collar seams, or a place where the seam will be turned within a facing. Work around each piece, putting them continuously through the sewing machine one after the other, following the instructions for continuous stitching in the next paragraph. (Skip this step if you're using a serger or pinked edges, since it'll be rather redundant.)

Then, in a similar assembly-line manner, stitch as many seams as possible in all sections of the garment. This may mean stitching both shoulder seams, the facing seams, around the collar, around the cuffs, etc., in one motion (Fig. 5–13). Pick up and join sections, stitching the seams continuously, moving from one to another without stopping in between. If you want to secure the

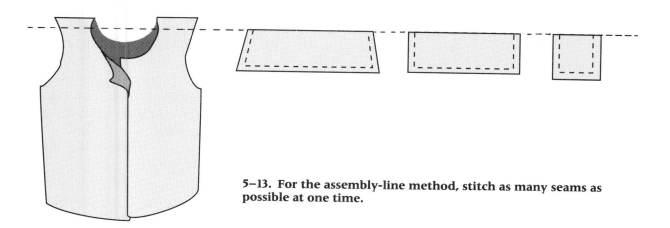

5–13. For the assembly-line method, stitch as many seams as possible at one time.

end of a seam, simply backstitch a couple times and then continue sewing. When you've joined as many sections as possible, move from the construction area to the pressing surface and press the seams. After this initial stitching and pressing, go back to the sewing machine and continue putting the garment together, doing all possible seams in one sitting before returning to the pressing surface. As you work through this process, there are fewer and fewer sections to be joined and the garment gradually comes to completion. It requires some forethought to pin the units together and run them through the machine continuously, but the time savings can be significant. After several experiences using this method, it will become second nature, as following the pattern instructions did when you began sewing.

## The Flat Construction Method

To briefly outline the flat construction method, the main objective is to do as much detailed work as possible on each garment section before joining them together. Because the sections are flat or smaller than the whole unit, it's easier to complete details like pockets and collars or applying trims and appliqués. Basically what you want to do is finish small detail areas such as darts, zippers, straps, ties, and pockets on the main garment pieces first; then stitch any horizontal seam lines, including shoulder seams, yokes and waistlines; complete any major detail areas such as collars and facings; use one continuous seam to stitch the garment from the underarm down the side to the hem; insert the sleeves in their finished form with cuffs already in place; and finally, complete any finishing details such as hems or buttons. Wow! One whole project completed in a "brief" sentence. But, I'm sure you get my point and can see how much easier it would be to work. It makes more sense to totally complete units like sleeves before joining them to the main body of the garment. Why move all that extra bulk around under the needle? It's just as easy to produce any plackets, easing or gathering first, then stitch the side seam and join the cuffs, before stitching the shoulder seam. If the project has no cuffs, you can join the sleeves at the shoulder seams while the garment is still flat and finish off with a seam from the garment bottom up past the underarm seam and down to the end of the sleeve. Even easier! Some easy-to-sew patterns already use this method. When buying a pattern, check for this information on the instruction sheet. You might like to follow step-by-step instructions before experimenting on your own. However, any pattern can be adapted to this method, with a little reorganization (Fig. 5–14). Instead of following the pattern instructions exactly, read through them briefly, noting the units that could be completed before joining them to the main body. Divide the garment pieces into each of these units and stack them

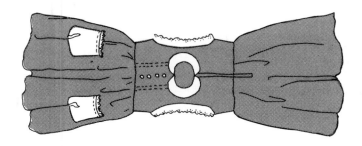

**5–14. The flat construction method on a dress. Detailed work is done before the garment is assembled, as much as possible.**

together. If you'd find it easier to have a checklist, make a note of the units and any special instructions you need to refer to. You can check off against this list as the units are finished. An example of this for a blouse, might include:

1. Stitch the outer seams of the collar and edge-stitch if desired.
2. Stitch the outer seams of the cuff and edge-stitch if desired.
3. Produce plackets, pleats, gathering, and easing on sleeve pieces as required. Stitch the underarm seams and attach cuffs. Turn cuff, hand-stitch the reverse side in place and mark buttonholes.
4. Add any appliqué, pockets, or special features to the front and back of the garment. If there are gathers or pleats, form these before joining the front and back with the yoke (if there is one) or before joining the front and back together at the shoulder seams. While the unit can be opened and laid flat, add the collar and facings. While it's still flat, it's easy to mark the buttonholes, make a test sample buttonhole, and stitch them. Stitch the buttonholes in cuffs also.
5. Stitch the side seams.
6. Insert the sleeves and press them in place.
7. Fold up the hems and stitch them in place by hand or by machine.
8. Complete any handwork, such as the placement of shoulder pads or buttons.

This method is very quick. It cuts down on the frustration of detailed work by giving you better access to the garment in its flat stage, but eliminates the intertangled pieces, which is an aspect of the assembly line method that some people hate. I'm sure that after trying this method you'll be more willing to add pleats, tucks, lace, appliqué or pocket details to projects.

## 9. FINISHING

After the garment has been constructed, only the finishing touches remain. You have very little work left before the project is complete. Earlier we talked about organization of project supplies. The remaining supplies should be near the construction surface or in the fitting area. Then you can simply reach out and sew on notions such as buttons and use a mirror for final placement of shoulder pads and hems before stitching them in place.

I used to complete garments up to this stage and then leave them. Often all they needed were buttons, but since I hadn't purchased them with the fabric or at the beginning of the project, I couldn't go any further. I'd recommend finishing a project and hanging it in your closet before beginning another one. After I'd spent several nights in a row doing hems, buttons, and fasteners on multiple garments, I adopted this philosophy. If you do, you'll sew and have something to wear. If you don't, you may sew but the closet will still be bare!

# Quilting

Along with making clothing, women in earlier days had to make bed coverings for the warmth and comfort of their families. Consequently, quilting was a big part of life years ago. While a young woman might make one or two bridal quilts, for the most part functional quilts were made, as they were necessary to keep the family warm throughout the long winter nights. Although practical, quilting also was perhaps the only creative outlet many women of that time had, and so their works evolved from purely functional creations into artistic ones. Quilting provided an opportunity for women to develop their skills and be creative; meeting over a quilt frame also allowed them the rare opportunity to socialize.

Today, women and men from all different avenues of life are quilting. Many enjoy the process of putting the quilt together; others enjoy mastering the procedure itself rather than the project. Still others like the color and texture of cloth and are fascinated by the multitude of impressions that can be achieved with this one medium.

Some quilts are hand-pieced and -quilted; others are machine-pieced and -quilted; some use a combination of both techniques. Anyone involved in the quilting world is aware of the constant battle over which is "true," hand or machine work. Whichever gives you the most satisfaction and allows you to be creative and artistic in your own way is right for you. When I began quilting several years ago, I self-righteously decided that I would only produce works done by hand. Years later, I have only one project stitched by hand, and that's a small crib quilt made for my son. I soon changed my attitude when I discovered the amount of work involved in producing one of those masterpieces. I realized I didn't have the time, the ambition, or the stick-to-it-ness required. So I tried machine quilting and quickly found out that just because it's done by machine doesn't mean it's easy. In fact, I think it's harder. Now, when I find that a particular point absolutely refuses to line up on a quilt, I combine hand and machine stitching in order to get the placement right. A combination of the two methods has worked for me to create the look I want.

Like the production of fashion garments, quilting projects can be organized into units. The better organized supplies and procedures are, the easier each step will become and the more enjoyable the overall project will be. I must admit that I've had a very difficult time writing this section of the book. Being totally addicted to quilting, I wanted to share with you every single detail I've learned that could possibly improve your skills or save you time. Some of them are simply going to have to be saved for another book, since this one focuses more on *what* to do versus *how* to do it. You can consult other books on speed-cutting and -piecing techniques; you'll learn some absolutely wonderful, incredibly quick and easy, and totally creative methods for producing artistic masterpieces.

## 1. THE DESIGN

Before you can begin to put the quilt together, familiarize yourself with the design and have a clear idea which fabric is going to go where. The most basic of patchwork quilts combines two fabrics, but as designs become more and more intricate, an infinite number can be used. Scrap quilts are often constructed using each fabric only once. To do this effectively, you need to know exactly what's going on.

When drafting designs, you want to create accurate, easy-to-follow patterns. If you have a computer there are two programs specifically designed for quilting that are worth looking into as of this writing. One is called The Electric Quilt and the other The Quilter's Design Studio. Both offer a variety of options for designing quilts. However, since the computer equipment and programs can run into the thousands of dollars and aren't always easily transportable, at some point you'll be making do with graph paper, a pencil, and a ruler.

Quality pencils, pencil crayons, erasers, sturdy rulers and an electric or battery-operated pencil sharpener are also essential. There are similar products on the market, so it would be worth your time to visit a stationery store and see what's available and feels the most comfortable to you.

Because I like to do a lot of designing and regard it as a take-along activity, I store my equipment together. If you don't have an appropriate bag or briefcase, a legal-sized envelope box (the kind that holds 500 envelopes) is just the perfect size and has the advantage of a removable lid. If you're without a hard surface to draw on, the lid provides a work table, while the box keeps everything together and close at hand. You don't have to open and close the lid every time you want something or spread it all out on the ground around you.

## 2. ORGANIZING SUPPLIES AND CHOOSING TOOLS

Are you choosing fabric for the design or a design for the fabric? Either way, you'll want to know how many fabrics are needed in total and how much of each. Nothing can be more discouraging than searching for the "perfect" combination, feeling good about your choices, and then going home to discover that you're short one or have to edit one out. Just as we check the pattern envelope to determine what notions are required in sewing clothing, we need to check the quilt diagram and instructions to get together everything for the project.

Not all quilt patterns provide summarized information on what to cut from which fabric. Some designers intermingle these instructions with the stitching instructions. That's great while you're sewing the quilt, but it can cause some problems when you're getting the supplies together. Working from the quilt diagram and the instruction sheet, make a Quilt Organization Checklist. List the fabrics numerically in order of use and note beside each the amount of fabric required (see Fig. 5–15 also). Collect the fabrics and cut small swatches of each. Tape each swatch next to its corresponding number on the Quilt Organization Checklist (page 113) and stack the actual fabrics in order of use. (If you haven't prewashed the fabrics, do that first.)

For all designs, but especially for your own originals, it's a good idea to recheck the diagram for the number of fabrics required and yardage. It is possible that one will accidentally be left out of the instructions. When I'm working on a design, I use a different-colored pencil for each fabric. Every time I use a new color on the drafted design, I also color a small square on a separate yardage sheet. This helps to keep track of the number of fabrics used, and I can refer to each color when figuring out the yardage and know that I'll have enough fabrics when I begin the project. Of course,

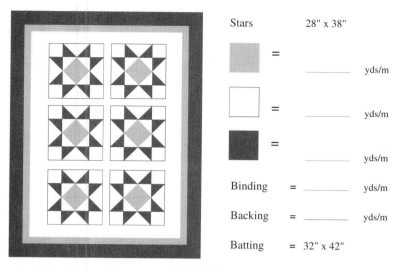

Stars          28" x 38"

[ ] = _____ yds/m

[ ] = _____ yds/m

[ ] = _____ yds/m

Binding   = _____ yds/m

Backing   = _____ yds/m

Batting   = 32" x 42"

**5–15. Quilting diagram and fabric list used to calculate yardage for shopping.**

the same system will work if you're using a black lead pencil and making different symbols or shades to represent each fabric.

It's not always possible to find those "perfect" fabrics all in one shopping spree. Several months ago I acquired a wonderful gold-embossed paisley with an electric blue in it and the perfect electric blue print to coordinate. However, the design I'm working with calls for three fabrics. The third fabric becomes the background of the previous two. After searching all our local stores. I've had to call a temporary halt to shopping sprees. The only color that will really blend them together well is a real gold background print, and I can't find one. So, I keep my shopping list in my purse. (Yes, it's a big purse!) When I come across a fabric I think might match, it can be verified against the samples on the list. You'll save a lot of money not buying the wrong fabric and a lot of time running back and forth between the store and home by carrying samples with you.

Shopping lists of this nature are a little more involved than a notation to buy "X" amount of a real gold background print. However, all you really need are samples of the other fabrics in the quilt. Tape a sample of each to an index card, note the name of the project and how many fabrics are used in total, a description of what you're looking for, and how much you need (Fig. 5–16). File these cards in a coupon pouch and carry them with you.

For a quilt, the quilt-top fabrics are definitely the main supplies needed, but there are others, such as needles, thread, batting, backing, and binding fabrics (if you didn't include them as one of the fabrics). Collect all the supplies, make sure you have everything, and then break down the package. The thread and

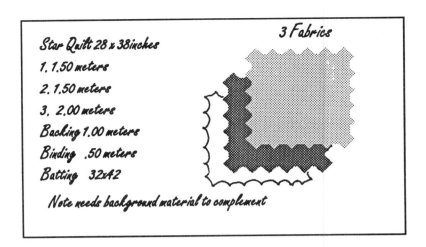

Star Quilt 28 x 38 inches
1. 1.50 meters
2. 1.50 meters
3. 2.00 meters
Backing 1.00 meters
Binding .50 meters
Batting 32x42

Note needs background material to complement

3 Fabrics

**5–16. A quilting shopping card.**

needles go to the construction area; the fabric, to the cutting surface; and the batting, backing, and bias fabrics to the finishing area. I simply store them at, near, or under the cutting surface where they won't be in the way, or in my storage closet if it will be quite a while before I require them. If you're an avid quilter, you may have one box to contain the supplies for each project you are working on.

Quilting has its own set of tools that are critical in all stages of cutting, construction and finishing. In other words, they're essential supplies. I've listed some below; additional ones may be required, depending on the design or technique used.

**1. Rotary Cutter:** This is the greatest tool ever invented for quilters, in my opinion. It has changed the face of quilting in an irreversible way. Even the boring procedures have become more fun. Cutters are available in various shapes and sizes (Fig. 5–17). I've heard it said that the larger sizes are easier to handle and control, but I haven't found this to be true for me. Experiment with different sizes to find which works better for you. People with smaller hands often find the large tools cumbersome and difficult to hold; those with large hands may find the small ones hard to hang on to.

**2. Replacement Blades:** Maintain a supply of replacement blades. Most fabric stores aren't open late. If you're in the middle of a project and don't want to quit, the lack of a fresh blade can be extremely frustrating. When the blade becomes nicked, it will skip threads along the cut, causing snags between the strips you are cutting. The cutting lines then will no longer be clean. It's tedious and annoying going back to snip these two or three threads that are skipped at regular intervals across the length of the fabric, so having replacement blades is a good idea.

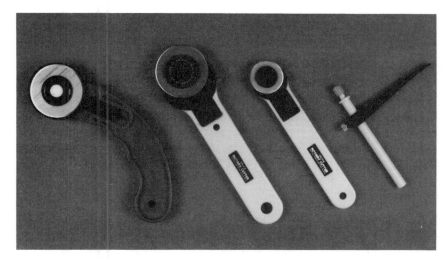

5–17. Several sizes and styles of rotary cutter. The tool on the right is an attachment for adding the seam allowance. Photo courtesy of Clotilde, Inc.

**3. Ruler:** The number of different shapes and sizes of rulers on the market is mind-boggling. Many have been created for specific projects or purposes. If you're following a designer's instructions and a specific tool is listed, often an address is given where the tool can be purchased.

What's needed on a regular basis is a tool that allows you to accurately measure and cleanly cut strips in combination with the rotary cutter. Some rulers come with black grids (Fig. 5–18). Others have yellow grids (Fig. 5–19). It's a matter of preference, so I recommend trying both types out. If you find a lot of color confusing you might prefer the black lines. On the other hand, if you like high contrast or have poor eyesight, you might like the yellow lines. Try both for yourself and see which you prefer.

A 6″ × 24″ ruler made of ¼″-thick clear plastic will meet the cutting requirements of most projects. Choose one marked in ⅛″ increments, which also has 45° and 60° angles marked on it. Additional perpendicular intersecting lines help you to make square cuts when cutting strips into pieces. They are also used for squaring borders or sub-cutting strips into individual shapes. Most of these rulers are also available in 12″ lengths. If you find the 24″ length too long, try the shorter one. It's more accurate to work with a ruler that reaches from one edge to the other of the fabric length being cut, however. An assortment of triangles and squares—4″, 6″, 8″, 12″, and 15″—is helpful for ensuring that quilt sections are properly shaped and completely squared up before joining them together. They are also used for cutting borders or dividing large pieces into smaller ones (see Fig. 5–20).

**4. Rotary Cutting Mat:** The rotary cutting mat is a forgiving surface that protects the blade of the rotary cutter and the surface

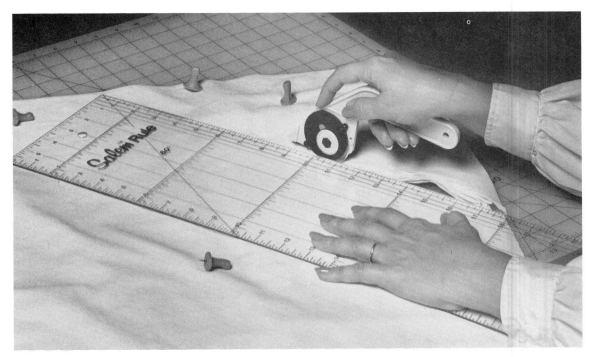

5–18. Using a rotary cutter with a transparent ruler. Photo courtesy of Salem Manufacturing Company, Ltd.

5–19. Squaring up a piece of fabric on a gridded ruler with a rotary cutter. Photo courtesy of Omnigrid, Inc.

**5–20. Cutting triangles, using a rotary cutter and gridded triangle. Photo courtesy of Omnigrid, Inc.**

of the cutting table. They come in an infinite range of sizes for almost any possible purpose. Some mats, such as those produced by Omnigrid,®are two-colored (Fig. 5–21). This allows you to use the side of the mat that provides the greatest contrast to the fabric, making cutting easier on your eyes. Mats can be purchased with or without gridded surfaces. If you're left-handed, pay special attention to the markings. Not all are manufactured for right- *and* left-handed use. All Omnigrid products are designed for left- and right-handed use, and their mats can be purchased with metric measurements, if you're more familiar with those.

Purchase a mat that is at least 18″ by 24″, to allow you to cut fabric as it comes off the bolt. Smaller ones are useful in classroom situations, but often, after you have used the larger size, you'll find them awkward. If you have a large cutting surface, consider getting a rotary mat that will cover the entire surface. These are available from most companies that produce mats or craft and cutting tables.

Take the time to work with the rotary cutting tools and get used to their feel. Learn how to use the tools accurately and efficiently to cut straight strips. As with any tool, repeated practice leads to greater familiarity and easier usage. There are several books that explain how to use these tools for speed-cutting. Quilt shops usually offer classes on what I term "the use and abuse of the rotary cutter." These aren't difficult tools to use, but they require

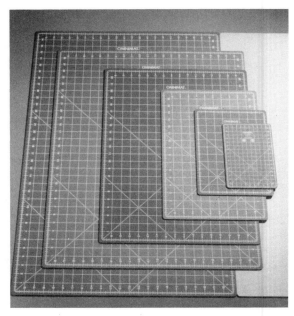

**5–21. Various sizes of rotary cutter mats. Photo courtesy of Omnigrid, Inc.**

some initial practice. They're fairly expensive to purchase but definitely worth every penny in time savings. Ask to try out a demonstration model at a shop, or get a friend to show you how his or hers works. Before you know it, you'll have them too!

It took only one small demonstration for me to add these "absolutely essential" tools to my wish list. I must have described their wonderful and varied uses in great detail, because my husband went out and purchased the whole ensemble for me relatively soon after that!

### 3. PRETREATING FABRICS

So far, I've been advocating pretreating fabrics and marking them with a small corner clip when you bring them home. Many of you have probably been panicking because you don't like to pretreat yours. It's true that some fabrics, such as polished cottons, are much crisper and easier to work with before pretreating than after. Also, quilting fabrics that are not pretreated tend to stretch less and handle better. It's not absolutely necessary to prewash quilt fabrics, but all the fabrics for one project should either *be* preshrunk, or else all should *not* be preshrunk. If some are and some aren't, the first time the completed project is laundered, it will become distorted by shrinkage in some areas and not others.

If you're producing quilts or quilted projects for resale, the finished product will have a much crisper, more professional look if you don't pretreat the fabric. However, I always worry about the buyers' reactions the first time they wash the quilt and everything shrinks and goes limp. To avoid this dilemma, prewash the fabric and then use a spray starch to iron the body back into the fabric before beginning construction. You get the best of both worlds!

## 4. CONSTRUCTION

Construction of a quilt top encompasses cutting, stitching, and pressing procedures. With the new techniques being developed, the division between these functions has changed. What follows is a brief overview of what can be accomplished. There simply isn't enough room in this book to provide you with all the details, but I want to give you an idea of the possibilities available so you can research them further.

### Placing Fabrics on Grain

Before cutting any shapes, place the fabric on grain. This isn't the old kind of on-grain that required pulling a thread and then stretching and forcing the fabric to conform. Instead, "on grain" now refers to close grain. The end result is to get clean, straight cuts at a 90° angle to the selvedge. Start by folding the fabric in half straight across, selvedge to selvedge (Fig. 5–22a). Don't worry if the non-selvedge ends are not even. They probably won't be, but will be trimmed with the first cut. You're more concerned that the fabric is folded straight across so that there aren't any ripples in the fold. Then, take the folded edge of the fabric and fold it up and straight across to meet the selvedges (Fig. 5–22b). Smooth out the fabric again, ensuring that there are no ripples along the new fold line. There are now four layers of fabric. The last fold line is the one measured against to get clean, straight cuts (Fig. 5–22c).

After folding the fabric, lay a square along the last (bottom) fold. Place the right side of a ruler against the left edge of the square, with one of the horizontal lines of the ruler along the fold of the fabric. The right edge of the ruler should be positioned to trim off the uneven edges of the fabric, but trim off as little as possible while still squaring up the fabric. Remove the square and hold the ruler firmly in place while you use the rotary cutter to make one slice along the ruler edge, trimming off the uneven edge of the fabric. This first cut is critical, as every subsequent one is measured from it (Fig. 5–22d).

Now you're ready to cut the required number and widths of strips. Again, place one horizontal line of the ruler along the bottom fold of the fabric. Measure along the ruler the width of the first strip, slide the ruler in place, and slice across the fabric

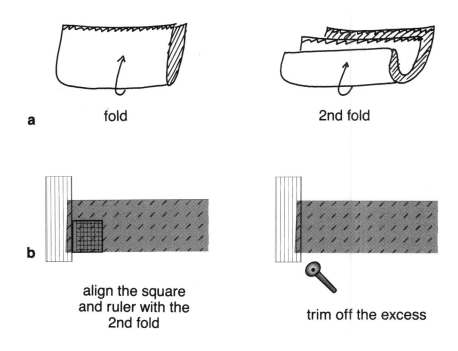

a    fold                          2nd fold

b    align the square
     and ruler with the
     2nd fold

     trim off the excess

**5–22. a. Folding fabric prior to cutting. b. Squaring up the fabric with a square and ruler, and trimming off the uneven ends.**

along the ruler edge, using the rotary cutter. Make as many strips as necessary with this first fabric before moving on to the next one. (These directions assume you're right-handed and cut from left to right. If you're left-handed you'll be reversing the order, measuring, and cutting from right to left.)

Place each fabric on grain as you work with it, and avoid moving fabrics around more than necessary. If you place them all on grain, stack them, and cut strips, this makes three steps instead of just one. Handle each as little as possible.

## Cutting Pieces

Previous to the invention of the rotary cutter, each shape was drawn onto the fabric, the ¼″ seam allowance was added around each, and then each piece was cut out individually. Some people tried stacking the fabrics and cutting more than one layer at a time, but it wasn't extremely accurate or easy to do. Even if you intend to hand-stitch the quilt-top together, you'll find it much easier to cut multiple pieces at one time than to repetitively cut shape after shape. Any shape desired—squares, diamonds, triangles, rectangles, whatever—can be more accurately cut using rotary equipment (Fig. 5–23).

After you have cut strips, the strips can be cut into smaller shapes. Lay the strip horizontally across the mat and slice across

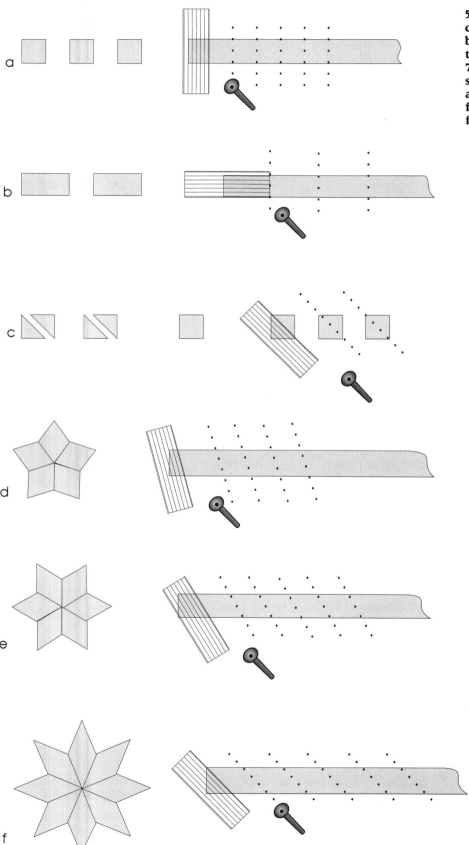

**5–23.** Using a rotary cutter to cut various shapes: a, squares; b, rectangles; c, right triangles; d, diamonds with 72° angles for 5-pointed star; e, diamonds with 60° angles for 6-pointed star; f, diamonds with 45° angles for 8-pointed star.

a

b

c

d

e

f

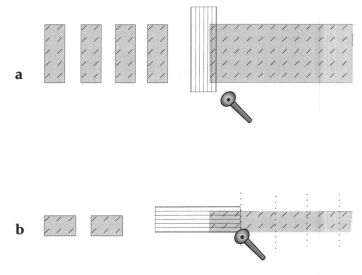

**5–24. Cutting rectangles with a rotary cutter: a, cut strips; b, sub-cut the strips into rectangles.**

at regular intervals, using the appropriate line or angle on the ruler to get the shape required (Fig. 5–24). For example, if you require forty 2″ × 5″ rectangles, don't cut out 40 individually. Instead, cut five 2″ × 45″ strips, then cut along each strip at 5″ intervals (8 cuts per strip) until 40 rectangles are made. Better yet, layer all 5 strips one on top of the other and make 8 cuts at 5″ intervals through all the strips simultaneously. With 13 cuts (including the ones to make the strips), you have the 40 rectangles. This is definitely a lot quicker than cutting one rectangle at a time.

Multiple strips of different colors also can be cut by layering the fabrics. This is similar to cutting out more than one garment at a time. A little more organization is needed, since the same number of strips may vary for each fabric. It's a little easier with fashion garments, where the same number of pattern pieces are cut out of each fabric. Suppose you need three 2″ strips of fabrics A, B and D and four 2″ strips of fabric E. Instead of cutting strips from each fabric individually, they can be stacked, and 3 strips can be cut from the entire group. Then fabric E can be removed, and an additional strip can be cut from it.

It's sometimes a good idea to make a quick-cutting chart, if one isn't provided with your quilt pattern. Make headings across the top for the different sizes of strips to be cut, and then note beside each fabric how many strips are required. Tape a small sample of each fabric in the margin. This will help to prevent any costly cutting errors. Cut the widest strip first, decreasing in size, cutting the narrowest width last. This way, if you accidentally cut too many wide strips, they can be cut down to the narrower size.

# QUILT ORGANIZATION CHECKLIST

Pattern: _____ Finished Size: _____
Source: _____
Number of Fabrics Required: _____
Backing: _____ Batting: _____ Thread: _____

**Fabric Swatch:**                    **Cutting Requirements:**

1.

2.

3.

4.

5.

6.

5–25a. A ¼″ sewing machine foot, used for accurately piecing quilt-tops. Photo courtesy of Little Foot, Ltd.

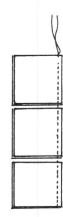

5–25b. Chain-piecing eliminates the need to start a new thread each time you start piecing a new pair of pieces.

You can't put it back on but you can cut off extra. (Wish that worked with weight too!) Start practicing this method on quilts that have same-sized strips—for example, Bargello, Log Cabin, Nine-Patch or Trip Around the World.

### Stitching

The standard seam allowance used in quilt construction is ¼″. Some machines come with a foot this width, or you can purchase one (Fig. 5–25). Some quilt instructors recommend just using the edge of the presser foot throughout as a guide and claim that because of this standard the project will work out. Sometimes it does, but other times it doesn't, especially in situations where one block has more seams and intricacies than the one it's being stitched to. Why take the chance? Because of that I recommend using a ¼″ foot. Little Foot (shown in Fig. 5–25a) is an extremely valuable tool. Not only does it enable you to stitch ¼″ seams perfectly, but it comes with ¼″ marks in front of and behind the needle, which aids in keeping accurate seam allowances on turns.

A variation of the continuous stitching method described for fashion projects is used by quilters and referred to as *chain piecing*. In chain piecing, many pairs of pieces are joined without cutting the thread between the pairs until *after* they are joined, eliminating the need to start sewing anew with each piecing. A few extra stitches are made between the pieced units for cutting purposes (Fig. 5–25b).

Returning to the project at hand, now that all your pieces are cut out, separate them into piles laid out in the same way as your block will be. Use chain-piecing methods to build your blocks in a shorter-than-usual time. Let's follow the example shown in Figure 5–26 to see how this is done.

1. First make the two-triangle squares, following the stitch-then-cut method described below.

2. Then lay out the pieced and solid squares that comprise a block in the order and orientation they will take in the block (Figure 5–26, bottom left). Stack the units repetitively on top of those for the first block.

3. Stitch the squares together in groups of two, beginning with square a and square b. Continue chain-piecing all of the square a units to all of the square b units until you have joined all the units you have in those two piles. Set them aside in their place.

4. Next, take one of square c and stitch it to square d. Repeat this for all the squares c and square d in the c and d piles.

5. Continue this method of joining single squares into units of two squares until they are all joined.

6. Cut the stitches between the chain-pieced units, and press them.

7. Next, join the units of two into units of four, as shown in Figure 5–26, Sequence 2. Sew ab to ef, and sew all the other ab units to their ef units, using chain-piecing methods, until you don't have any more.

8. Repeat the joining of the twos into units of 4 squares until all the units of two are joined into units of 4. Cut the stitches between the chain-pieced units to separate them, and press them.

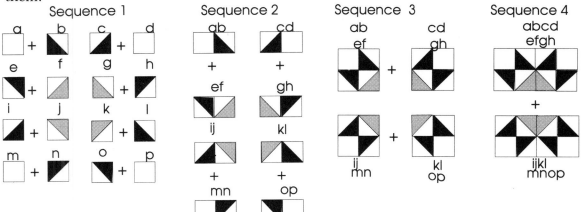

5–26. Making a quilt block by chain-piecing. After 2-triangle squares are made, square units are laid out in the order and direction they take in a block (Sequence 1) and groups of two squares are joined together. In Sequence 2 the 2-square units are joined to make 4-square units. In Sequence 3, the 4-square units are joined to make 8-square units. In Sequence 4, the block is made from 8-square units.

9. In the same way, sew the units of 4 squares together (see Figure 5–26, Sequence 3), until they are all combined. Cut the stitches between the chain-pieced units to separate them, and press them.

10. Sew a unit of 8 squares to another unit of 8 squares (Figure 5–26, Sequence 4) to complete a block. Repeat for all the blocks. When you've finished all the stitching procedures, all the blocks are complete, not just one!

You'll find it difficult to make just one block at a time after trying this method. The thought process is so much more complicated when you have to think through each seam instead of simply picking up the next stack and continuously stitching the units together.

## Stitch-Then-Cut Method

By stitching before cutting, a major amount of work can be completed in a short time. If you could stitch 96 groups of two triangles together to form pieced squares, prior to cutting them out, using one continuous seam, in roughly 20 minutes, would you? Of course you would! But believe it or not, this is one of those methods that people put off trying until they've actually seen it work. I have to admit that I did it myself.

Often triangles and strips can be stitched together before they are cut into the various shapes needed for the quilt. By stitching first and cutting later, you avoid overworking the fabric or, in the case of triangles, working with bias edges. This increases the accuracy of each piece, as they are handled less and are therefore less likely to loose their shape. Considerably fewer seams need to be stitched, and the quilt-top is produced accurately with increased speed.

The general gist of how it works is that two fabrics are pressed with right sides together, a grid is drawn on the fabric of squares equal to the finished pieced square plus the extra for the seam allowance, and diagonal lines are drawn to intersect the grid in both directions. These cutting lines are used as a seam guide. Following the cutting lines, one continuous seam is stitched around the grid ¼″ on either side of the cutting lines (Fig. 5–27). The units are cut apart on the cutting lines. When they are cut apart, there are triangles of two fabrics sewn to each other, forming a square. The stitching method differs, depending on the type of triangle desired.

The diagrammed method shown in Fig. 5–27 is for making half-square triangles. (Note: because of the triangular shape of the finished pieces the seam allowance added is not the traditional ¼″ but ⅞″.)

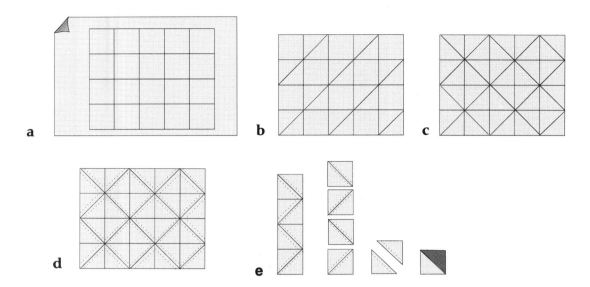

**5–27. Stitch-then-cut method for 2-triangle squares. a: A grid is drawn on the fabric of squares equal to the finished size of the pieced square plus an extra amount for the seam allowances. b, c: The diagonal cut lines are drawn between the corners of the squares. d: The triangles are stitched ¼" on either side of the cut lines. e: The units are cut apart on the cut lines and pressed open (extreme right).**

There are other methods that vary these instructions to some degree, or which are totally different. However, they all use rotary equipment, strip piecing, and speed cutting techniques. As you get more involved with quilting, continue to look through books for new and improved methods. There's always something new to learn.

There's an even quicker way to make half-square triangles using a gridded paper product, such as Triangle Paper for Quilters®. This is a paper product with the grid and stitching lines already marked. You simply pin the paper to the fabric, stitch as directed following the arrows, cut apart on the solid lines, tear off the paper, and press. You form triangles quickly and accurately without the need to draw a grid yourself.

When making pieced blocks, such as 4-patch and 9-patch designs, it's easiest to sew two or three strips together, press them, and then cut the strips into units of pieced blocks (see Fig. 5–28). Instead of cutting up thousands of little squares and sewing them together, cut, stitch, and sub-cut strips of fabric, which minimizes marking, sewing, and cutting.

Imagine the design calls for twenty 4-patch blocks. The working width of the fabric is 40". One choice is to cut forty 2" squares from fabric A and forty 2" squares from fabric B, sew one individual square of fabric A to one of fabric B with 40 small, short seams, press the 40 seams, and resew 20 AB blocks to 20 BA

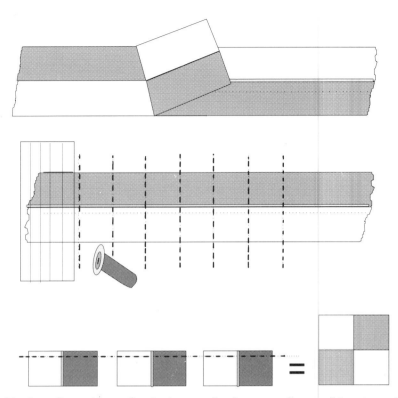

**5–28. Speed-cutting and -piecing methods streamline making 4-patch blocks. a: Two pieced strips are placed, with right sides together, as shown. b: With a ruler, slices are made at intervals across the pieced strips with a rotary cutter. c: Two-square units are chain-pieced to each other to create 4-patch blocks like the one at the right.**

blocks with 20 slightly longer seams. Have you envisioned how much work is involved? Now imagine this method: Sew a strip of fabric A to a strip of fabric B; sew another strip of fabric A to another strip of fabric B. Press the seam allowances towards the darkest fabrics. Lay the strips with right sides together and seam allowances butting, with the darker fabric of one of the strips positioned over the lighter one of the underneath strip. Make 20 cuts at 2″ intervals across the length of the joined strips (see Fig. 5–28). Pick up each pair of units, and stitch them together into a 4-patch design, using chain-piecing techniques, and press. You've completed twenty 4-patch blocks with only two long seams and 20 short ones. Much easier! Use the same method when making 9-patch blocks or other blocks where there are repetitious shapes that could easily be sewn in strips first and then cut.

## 5. MARKING

Before marking the quilt-top, make sure the corners are squared properly (Fig. 5–29) and press the top well. Clip away any

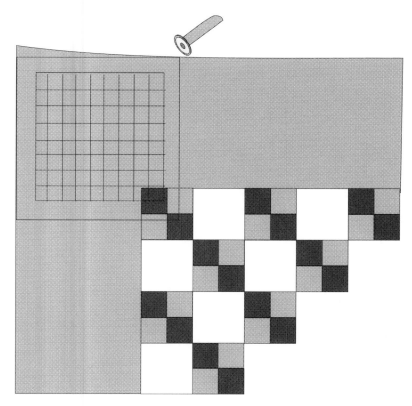

**5–29. Squaring up a quilt top's corner, using a gridded square and rotary cutter.**

unnecessary bulk within the seam allowances and remove all loose or long threads attached to the quilt-top front or back. Be careful that no accordion pleats have formed on the back.

Just as with fashion sewing, there are numerous marking tools available for quilting. Choosing a suitable one can be difficult. Always consider the method required to remove the markings and pretest on scraps of fabric to make sure the marks really wash out of the fabric you plan to use it on. Different fabrics will react differently to the same marking tool. You may be able to use a marker on all the fabrics but one in the quilt-top, for example. By testing you will know this before it's too late and the quilt top is ruined.

The most common marker is a graphite pencil. A #4H (hard) lead pencil works best, because the point stays sharper longer and a very light line can be drawn. Avoid #2 soft lead pencils, as cotton fabrics tend to absorb the line and often it can't be removed later. If you're looking for a refillable pencil that is always sharp, never smears, and produces a narrow, consistent line width that can be covered with thread during stitching and washes out, it is marketed under the name of Ultimate Marking Pencil (Fig. 5–30).

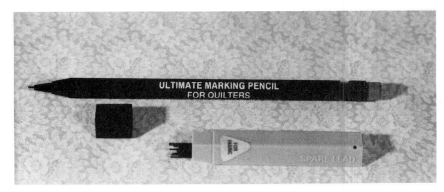

5–30. A refillable marking pencil for quilters. Photo courtesy of Ultimate Marking Pencil.

Marking a quilt can be quite tedious. The markings must be accurate, visible and not too dark. However, the markings are extremely important to achieving the overall effect of the quilt. Quilting lines should be smooth and flow together. Cross-hatching should be even and perpendicular. Patterns along borders should round the corner without becoming disjointed or uneven.

You may decide to avoid marking altogether by using a stencil paper like EZ Stitch Thru Stencils. This is a durable but flexible paper with preprinted quilting designs. Simply pin the paper to the fabric, stitch following the continuous lines, and tear the paper away (Fig. 5–31). Because the paper is translucent and has printed centering marks, accurate placement can be assured. If you'd prefer to create your own design rather than using one of the preprinted ones, blank stencil papers are available.

Cross-hatching is a very attractive, frequently used quilting pattern. However, the whole effect can be ruined if the markings aren't even. Latch-hook rug canvas has evenly woven squares that can be used to create a stencil through which markings can be made onto the quilt top. Because it's available by the yard in most craft stores, just about any size stencil can be made. Evenly mark the cross-hatch grid onto the latch-hook canvas using a felt-tip pen and then lay it over the quilt top. Make quilting lines by pushing a marker through the canvas holes, following the pattern, leaving a line of dots on the quilt top. Stitch along the dotted lines.

An alternative to cutting stencils is to use a light box or table, a transparent surface with a light source below it. Because it's so simple, this tool is useful for all sizes of projects from small pillows to large quilt projects; it's also quick and easy. A light table can be set up using a lamp and glass surface. Glass coffee or dining room tables work very well, or simply open an expanding table and cover the gap with a sheet of glass. Remove the lampshade and place the lamp on the floor below the glass. Draw the quilting pattern onto paper using a bold, dark line and tape it to the glass. Lay the quilt top over the light box and pattern and transfer the markings. Higher wattage bulbs will make it easier to trace lines onto dark fabrics. Needless to say, don't leave this setup when small children have access to your work area without supervision, as it could be quite dangerous.

If you need to use a light table frequently, a temporary one like the one described above can be extremely frustrating—like reverting back to sewing on the kitchen table. You need something a little more practical. Me Sew, Inc., produces a lightweight, portable light box (Fig. 5–32). Fluorescent lighting is placed below the box and the quilt design is taped to the top. The fabric is placed above. The light shines through all layers, allowing for easy transfer of the quilting design. Light boxes are usually available from graphic supply houses, as they are used by commercial artists also. It's amazing how many uses can be found for a light box beyond marking quilts, once you've got one.

## 6. BASTING

Basting is another one of the steps between piecing the quilt top and quilting the layers. In order to create a quilt there has to be a quilt-top, batting, and backing. The three layers of this "sandwich" are held together with basting, which temporarily holds the three layers firmly together to avoid their slipping or stretching, while you quilt. The basting is removed after quilting

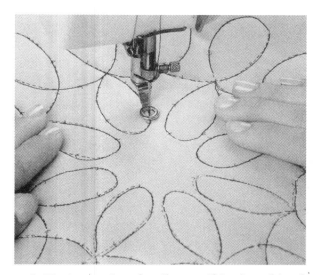

5–31. A preprinted quilt stencil is pinned in place and used instead of marking the quilt top. The quilter stitches right through the paper (a) and tears it away (b). Photo courtesy of EZ International.

**5–32. Three sizes of light box. Photo courtesy of Me Sew, Inc.**

**5–33. Two methods of basting. Left, pin basting; right, basting with thread. Both start from the center and work outwards.**

is complete. Basting is done with safety pins or with a traditional running stitch (Fig. 5–33). With either method, begin basting from the center of the quilt; work towards the outside edges, smoothing and gently easing the quilt-top into place as you work.

Many of us have stretched and basted a quilt on the floor, using traditional methods. Instead of using the floor, prevent an aching

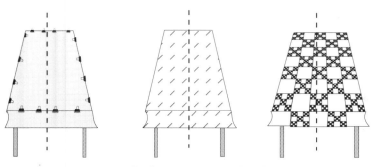

**5–34. Preparation for basting. Left: clip the backing to your work surface with binder clips, face-down. Middle: center the batting on top. Right: center the quilt top, face up, over the batting.**

back and sore knees by using a surface approximately 3′ wide × 5′ long; for example, a sheet of plywood, counter top, or tabletop. Raise the height of the surface until you are comfortable—usually it will be about waist height—by placing wooden blocks or books underneath.

Center and stretch the quilt backing face-down across the surface, using binder clips to hold it in place. As you stretch the fabric taut, simply slide the clip onto the edge of the surface to hold it firmly in place. Layer the batting and quilt top over the backing, centering each layer progressively (Fig. 5–34). The quilt top is face-up. If the quilt top is bigger than your work surface, baste it in sections from the middle out, shifting and reclipping the backing as you work.

Pins provide the quickest method for basting the surface. Approximately 300 to 500 #1 nickel-plated safety pins are needed for an average-sized quilt. These are 1″ long with fine tips that will not damage the fabric. #0 pins are finer and smaller and, if you can find them in bulk, are even easier to use. Nickel pins are used because they won't rust and leave black marks in the fabric like brass ones can. The success of the quilting depends not only on how well stretched the layers are but how securely they're held together. Quilting is much easier when the layers can be controlled and prevented from shifting. With cotton batting, the pins should be placed 3″ to 4″ apart; with polyester batting, they must be much closer together, about 2″ to 3″ apart. The pins will stay in the quilt while it's rolled and re-rolled during the quilting process, so be generous and don't skimp with the number used.

Whether you prefer to baste with traditional running stitches or with pins, there are several ways to preserve your fingers from constant pricking and to keep your nails from breaking. As you're bringing the needle/pin back up and out of the layers, press the edge of a basting spoon against the surface at the location where the needle will emerge (see Fig. 5–35). Then draw the needle up

**5–35. A basting spoon, used with pin or thread basting. Photo courtesy of Cottage Mills, Inc.**

into the spoon's grooved curve, where it can easily be picked up. Your fingers will thank you!

Two other available basting tools are the Kwik Klip and Needle-Ez. The Kwik Klip tool is used to close safety pins as they emerge from the layers. The pin rides on the ridge of the tool, and you simply push the pin closure down and click the safety pin together. The Needle-Ez tool replaces a thimble and helps to push needles through thick materials or areas with seams.

When you use a running stitch for basting, be very careful about stretching and clamping the backing fabric down. Make sure there will be no extra fullness once the basting is completed. It's not as easy to remove the basting stitches and redo them as it is to redo the pin basting. Not that we want to redo anything!

## 7. PACKAGING FOR QUILTING

Take time to package the layers before you move on to machine quilting. Don't just grab the quilt and start shoving the bulk under the needle, because you'll quickly run into complications. Distortion is caused when the batting is pushed in too many directions, so you want to avoid turning the quilt under the machine as much as possible. A large quilt is difficult, if not impossible, to turn through the 9″ opening in a machine. It's easiest to work with only half of the quilt under the machine at a time, keeping the remainder rolled, packaged, and contained so its bulk won't create difficulties.

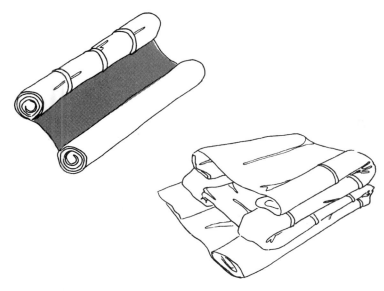

**5–36. Left: The basted quilt sides are rolled up prior to machine quilting, and secured with quilt clips. Right: A method of folding the quilt while it is rolled, so it can be machine quilted.**

Quilting traditionally begins in the center of the quilt, moving first to the right edge and then to the left. Roll each side of the quilt inward, stopping within 2″ of the center. As the right side will gradually be unrolled, it can be loosely clipped together, but since you don't want the left side unrolling at all, it must be firmly held in place. Quilt clips will secure even a fairly bulky roll (Fig. 5–36). These are U-shaped and rounded, and are manufactured out of plastic. As well as being snag-free, they provide sufficient spring action to contain the quilt's bulk. On average, four to twelve clips are needed for a large quilt. The clips are available in two sizes, a 2″ size for crib quilts and smaller wall hangings as well as a 3″ full size (Fig. 5–37). Since the clips are made of plastic, there is no need to cover them with twill tape to avoid scratching the machine.

After rolling and securing the quilt, fold it again in a zigzag, accordion fashion from end to end, forming a compact package (see Fig. 5–36, right). This will sit on your lap and automatically will unfold as you work. The quilt should be going down into the machine, not dragging up from your lap, so you'll need to unfold portions as you work to create height. When you've finished quilting the right roll portion of the quilt, rotate the quilt 180°, and roll and repackage it again. Continue stitching along the length, progressing from the center out to what is now the right edge (formerly the left edge) again.

When you've finished quilting one length and are ready for the next quilting line, simply unroll within the clips. Don't remove them each time. Diagonal quilting lines require the same

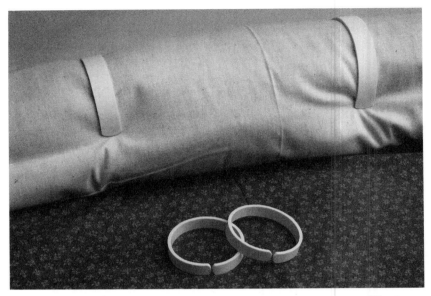

5–37. Two sizes of quilt clips. Photo courtesy of Cottage Mills, Inc.

packaging technique, except the quilt is rolled in from opposite corners instead of from the sides.

## 8. MACHINE QUILTING

### Planning

You've reached the final stages of the quilt project and are more than likely quite anxious to see it finished. Don't rush. Not even if you're close to a deadline! There is no substitute for quality workmanship in any step of the quiltmaking process. Perhaps you have machine-pieced a quilt but are planning to hand-quilt it. Since this book deals with ways to organize projects for greater speed and production, I would recommend machine-quilting as the faster method, even though it requires as much if not more practice than traditional hand-quilting in order to produce even, precise stitching.

For machine-quilting, plan the quilting stitches in advance so you can work around the quilt in a uniform manner, using one continuous line of stitching where possible. Straight-line and free-motion quilting can be combined. The entire project needs to be planned to make smooth transitions between each of these areas. It is helpful to have a diagram of the quilt. If you've been working an original design, take a few minutes to sketch a rough diagram and lightly pencil in the planned quilting lines. Total accuracy in detail is not necessary; you simply need to know what is going to go where. With dotted lines or small arrows, show the direction

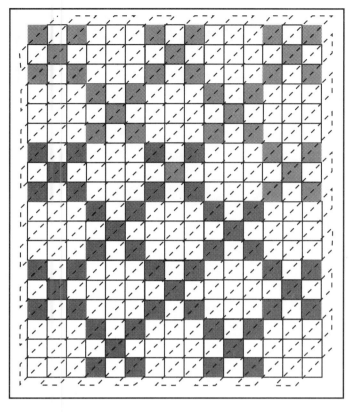

**5–38. A sketch helps plan quilting lines for machine quilting.**

the stitching lines will follow (Fig. 5–38). Plan a route that allows you to work from one area of the quilt to another with as many continuous stitching lines as possible. Stitching in the ditch (stitching along the seam line) can be used to work across small unconnected areas. With larger quilts, you may find it easier to mentally divide the quilt top, similar to the way it will be packaged to actually quilt, and work out the stitching flow within each division.

## Straight-Line Quilting

Stitching in the ditch is the most common form of straight-line quilting. Since it's not a decorative technique, it's often used for quilts that don't require fancy surface quilting. This stitch is a functional method of securing the three layers together and anchoring the layers between the blocks before completing fancier surface quilting designs within the blocks. Quilting or stitching in the ditch will stabilize the quilt and make it more controllable under the machine's foot.

Usually stitching in the ditch is done with a walking foot (Fig. 5–39), which helps to ease the bulk of the layers under the needle smoothly so there's less chance of tucking on the back or

5–39. A walking foot and ruffler. Photo courtesy of Clotilde, Inc.

5–40. Stitching in the ditch.

front of the quilt and stitches are more evenly spaced. When the quilt top was pieced, the seam allowances were pressed in one direction, which makes a high and low side to the seam. To stitch in the ditch, stitching is placed along the length of the seam, with the needle on the lower side just against the seam ridge (Fig. 5–40). After stitching is done, when the fabric relaxes, the stitches are hidden within the fold. (Note: The other attachment shown in Figure 5–39 is a ruffler. It gathers up the fabric for you, making ruffles on quilts, curtains, pillows, even skirts, a lot easier and quicker.)

## Free-Motion Quilting
Free-motion quilting is the newest form of machine quilting and has virtually freed the quilter by providing the ability to

reproduce almost any of the intricate designs used in hand-quilting. Small designs, sharp curves, and intricate patterns that can be difficult to stitch by hand are possible, and sometimes are easier to achieve by machine. Experimentation and practice are required, but your efforts will be rewarded.

The free-motion stitch is done by replacing the regular foot with a darning foot and dropping or covering the feed dogs on the machine. With the feed dogs lowered, you are in total control of the stitch. How fast you move the fabric and the speed of the machine combine to determine the stitch length as you stitch backwards, forwards, and side to side without turning the quilt. Imagine the freedom this represents! After you've tried this stitch, you'll probably find it's quite addictive. I know I just love to add the stippled textures to areas of my quilts. A Big Foot (Fig. 5–41) can be used in place of the darning foot. Its clear 1″ surface allows you to see what you're doing, where you're going, and where you've been. Because of its larger size, more contact is made with the quilt surface than is available with a standard darning foot.

Even straight-line stitching such as stitching in the ditch, cross-hatching, or grid quilting is possible using the "footless" free-motion method. By freely producing straight rows of stitches as well as curved ones, you have the ability to work each area completely from end to end, moving across the quilt. You aren't limited to doing all the straight stitches first and then the curved ones. If it weren't for the fact that the bobbin would run out of

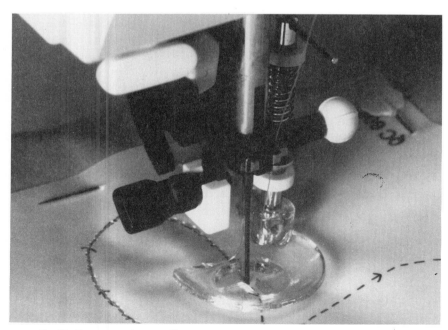

**5–41. Free-motion quilting, using a special foot called Big Foot. Photo courtesy of Little Foot, Ltd.**

thread, it would be possible to quilt an entire top with one continuous row of stitching!

Both stitching in the ditch and free-motion stitching require patience and practice to perfect. Start with samples at first, and then move from smaller to bigger projects. The unlimited number of possibilities that exist once you've mastered these techniques will encourage you. In every quilt you visualize or produce, you'll begin to see areas where these two techniques can be used not only to enhance the quilt, but to make production less time-consuming and boring, although still creative and artistic.

## 9. FINISHING TOUCHES

Once the quilting is done, all that's left is to finish off the quilt's edges. Some are finished with the "pillow method," in which the quilt-top and backing/batting are sewn together with right sides together, leaving a small opening through which to turn the quilt right-side out. The majority are completed with a turned bias binding, which is by far the more professional look, but the more time-consuming one.

### Binding

Self-fabric bindings can be made with very little effort. You can get approximately 16 yards of 2¼″ wide binding (unfolded width) from cutting, resewing, and pressing an entire yard of fabric. The expense for this small amount of fabric is minor compared to the look of binding perfectly matched to your fabric. You can make continuous binding, which saves time otherwise used in piecing sections together. Instructions are given below. You may find it easier to start by making continuous straight binding.

To make continuous straight binding:

1. Take a rectangle of the fabric you want to use, and mark equally spaced lines on the right side of the fabric, with the width of the unfolded bias binding between them, as shown in Fig. 5–42a.

2. With right sides of fabric together, pin the two short ends together, out of alignment, so that one width of the marked fabric is hanging out unmatched over the side of the other short end (Fig. 5–42b), and stitch the ends with ¼″ seam allowance.

3. Turn the fabric right-side out (Fig. 5–42c) and cut along the marked lines to make one continuous strip of straight binding.

To make continuous bias binding:

1. Take a square of the fabric you want to use and cut it on the diagonal (Fig. 5–43a) into two triangles.

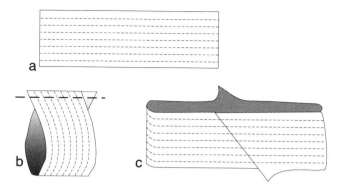

**5–42. Making continuous straight binding. See text for details.**

2. Overlap and seam the two triangles on a short side with the right sides of fabric facing and ¼″ seam allowances (Fig. 5–43b). Open up the fabric and press it.

3. On the right side of the fabric, mark equally spaced lines with the width of the unfolded bias binding you want between them, as shown in Fig. 5–43c.

4. Pin the two short ends of the fabric together with right sides facing, but shift the ends out of alignment so one width of the marked bias binding is hanging out over the side of the other short end. Seam the two ends together with ¼″ seam allowance (Fig. 5–43d). Turn the fabric right-side out.

5. Cut along the marked lines to form a continuous strip of bias binding (Fig. 5–43e).

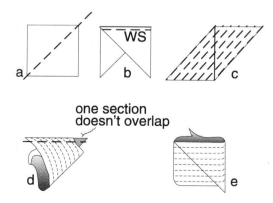

**5–43. Making continuous bias binding. See text for details.**

Before sewing the bias binding around the quilt edges, pin two rod pockets in place on the back of the quilt at the quilt's top and bottom. The one at the top will encase the rod for hanging the quilt; the one at the bottom will hold a rod that acts as a weight to keep the quilt hanging straight.

To make the rod pockets, cut a rectangle of fabric equal in length to the width of the quilt. The width of the rectangle should be double the width needed to fit the rod plus twice the seam allowance. Fold the corners of the rectangle up as shown in Fig. 5–44a on the wrong side of the fabric, making a 45° angle. Then fold and press the strip in half along its length (Fig. 5–44b). Position each pocket in place, with the raw edges aligned with the quilt's raw edge, on the back of the quilt (Fig. 5–44c). When the binding is sewn in place, the raw edges of the pockets will be caught within the seam allowances, leaving only the folded pocket edges to be hand-stitched to the backing. I've occasionally forgotten this step, but not very often. Doing four rows of hand-stitching has a way of reminding me! Since at some time in the future I may change the way I use a quilt, I put rod pockets on all of my quilts, even those that are originally intended for use on a bed.

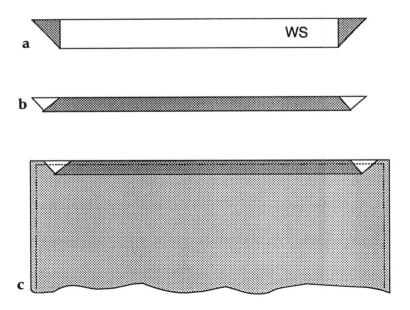

**5–44. Making and attaching a rod pocket. a: Fold the fabric corners up at 45° angles. b: Press the strip in half as shown. c: Stitch the strip in place along with the binding.**

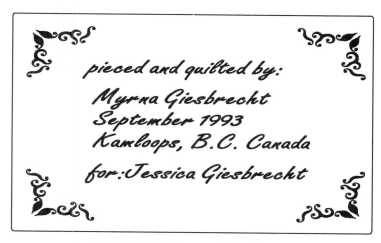

**5–45. A label for a quilt back.**

## Signing and Documenting Your Work

Always sign your work. Somewhere on the front or back of the quilt, embroider your name, the date, and your location onto the quilt. If you don't want to embroider the information in, have labels manufactured with this information, and sew one to the back of each quilt (see Fig. 5–45 for an example). Take a picture of the finished piece, and keep an album of your work. Note where, when, and why the quilt was made, for whom, and where it is now. Be proud of each masterpiece, whether it's your first or one hundred and
twenty-first.

## CONCLUSION

What I've presented is a library of organizational ideas and techniques that you can develop to improve the quality of your projects, while decreasing the amount of time needed to complete them. Since I am dealing with the "what to" more than the "how to" issue here (there is a subtle difference), you may find that you need further clarification of some techniques. Your local sewing shop probably offers a selection of courses, and may be open to suggestions for additional ones. Don't hesitate to ask if there is something you would like them to teach you. The techniques presented here may be totally new to some of you and old hat to others. Some you may have read about but never tried. I encourage you to try new techniques. Practice on scrap pieces of fabric or small projects. Each new skill mastered gives you an additional level of creativity to use in future projects.

Fear of the unknown sometimes hinders us from using the correct technique. Instead we make do with something easier. Stitching in the ditch was a method I used to avoid at any cost.

My level of perfectionism wouldn't allow me to have any stitches showing on the right side of the quilt, but my skill level meant I couldn't make the work look the way I wanted it to look. Instead of practicing and improving my skills. I'd continually stitch ¼″ from the seam allowance instead. For years I avoided trying to stitch in the ditch, although many projects would have benefited from hidden stitching. When a good-quality nylon filament thread became available, it allowed me to try the technique without fear of intolerable imperfections, and to perfect it to the point that I now stitch in the ditch somewhere on almost all quilts. I'm even using colored threads now instead of the invisible nylon!

Don't be afraid to try something new. When you're reading books and articles or attending seminars, always look for new techniques to develop and improve your skills, and ways to organize your project or sewing area more efficiently.

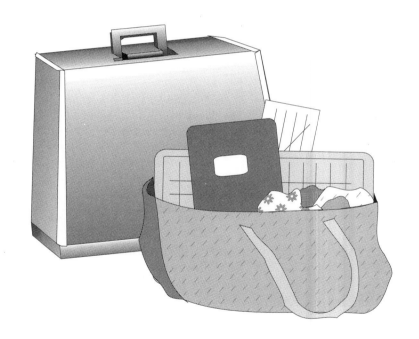

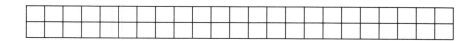

## · 6 ·

# Sew Far from Home: What to Pack

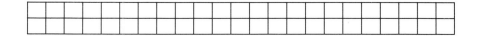

Have you ever signed up for a class, packed up all your supplies, thought and thought until you were sure that absolutely everything but the kitchen sink was in the bag and then arrived, set up, and discovered you'd forgotten something crucial like the foot pedal? Believe it or not, this has happened to more than just one person!

This chapter discusses tools that should be included in your class bag. If you prefer not to pack and unpack, these tools could remain in the bag: they would be used only in a classroom situation, and not in your sewing room. Tools purchased to remain in the class bag should be the same brand and style you use for work at home. Unless you attend classes on a regular basis, odd tools will not become familiar.

After teaching classes for several years, I devised a checklist of basic supplies that each student needed to bring. This basic list is the same for most classes. Any differences in supplies will be given in the actual class requirements. The checklist insures that all essential supplies arrive at the classroom with you. While a class should be educational, the lessons shouldn't be on "How To Do Without" or "Perfecting Your Borrowing Skills"! A copy of my Classroom Checklist is given on page 136. It contains the basic supplies used in most class situations. This checklist is useful not only to pack supplies for class, but also to insure they're all repacked and returned home.

When you attend a class, take as many personal sewing supplies as possible. I've discovered that work on a new project flows more smoothly when you use tools that are familiar and comfortable. In some cases, it's not practical to take your sewing machine, but other, smaller supplies are more transportable.

## 1. BASIC TOOLS

There are basic tools that are required for every sewing class.

# CLASSROOM CHECKLIST

**Machine:**
- presser foot _____
- foot pedal _____
- bobbin _____
- bobbin case _____
- needles _____
- light bulb _____
- extension cord _____

**Cutting Tools:**
- shears _____
- thread snippers _____
- rotary cutter _____
- spare blades for cutter _____
- rotary cutting mat _____
- adhesive bandages _____

**Measuring Tools:**
- imperial/metric measuring tape _____
- seam guide _____
- rulers (regular, square, and triangle) _____

**Pins and Needles:**
- dressmaker's pins _____
- safety pins _____
- hand-sewing needles _____
- pin cushion _____

**Stitching Tools:**
- thread (piecing and quilting) _____
- seam ripper _____

**Writing Tools:**
- lined paper _____
- graph paper _____
- pen _____
- pencils _____
- colored pencils _____
- eraser _____
- correction fluid _____
- hole punch _____
- binder for pages _____

**Extra Supplies:**
- lunch bag or plastic bag for garbage _____
- transparent tape _____
- masking tape _____
- luggage carrier _____
- ironing surface _____
- iron _____
- water container _____
- electrical outlet bar _____
- calculator _____
- tickets _____
- lunch _____

Some of these are considered so basic that the instructor will not bother to note them on the supply list. If you don't receive a list, or if you think additional supplies may be required, ask for further information. Prepare for any eventuality (within reason) by taking anything you think you might need anyway!

**Sewing machine.** The primary tool in any class involving sewing is, of course, the sewing machine. Most of us probably think that it's pretty basic to pack up our machine and take it to class. However, there are a few essential parts that must be included but often are missed. Check to make sure you have not only included the foot pedal but also the presser foot, the bobbin case, bobbins, extra needles, and a light bulb. If your machine has a short electrical cord, include an extension cord. (This is often necessary even if the machine has a long electrical cord as the outlet may be on the other side of the room.) Since machines have a tendency to act up when removed from their familiar environment, it's a good idea to pack the instruction manual.

**Cutting tools.** There's a wide variety of cutting tools available. A good pair of regular cutting shears should be packed, as well as some small thread snippers. Shears and scissors need to be kept sharp to make clean, accurate cuts. A rotary cutter is useful in many classroom situations. Be sure to include spare blades and a rotary cutting mat. June Tailor, Inc., manufactures a board called the Cut'n Press that's perfect for classroom situations. Use one side along with rotary equipment to cut; then flip the board over and use the other side for pressing (Fig. 6–1).

**Measuring tools.** A measuring tape should be included. Take one that measures in inches and centimetres. The instructor may not use the same units of measure as you. A seam guide is useful for accurately measuring seam allowances. Rulers need to be packed for use with the rotary cutter. Many students prefer the 12″ length for classroom use because it's shorter, therefore easier to transport and in less danger of breaking than a long ruler.

**Pins.** Long, sharp, clean pins make pin-basting seams much easier. I prefer the extra-long dressmaker's pins. These are thin and will firmly baste the fabrics together before stitching. Take a box of pins, not just a few, as you'll have no idea of the pinning requirements. It's always better to be overprepared than underprepared. A pincushion, either the regular "tomato" style, a wrist variety, or a magnetized one, makes keeping track of pins easier. Safety pins may be needed for pin basting quilt projects or threading elastic. Include some hand-sewing needles as well.

**Thread.** Include a variety of thread colors. A fashion color will have been chosen to coordinate with your fabric, but some basic or blending colors—like white, black, ecru, grey, or peach—can also be packed and left in your carry bag. Prewind your bobbins. This will save a lot of valuable class time, and you'll be better prepared.

**Seam ripper.** Now, I know that we never make mistakes and won't need this tool but just in case the person *next* to you needs it, you should take a seam ripper! Many times in a classroom, when you're learning

**6–1. A Cut'n Press board is designed for rotary cutting on one side and pressing on the other. Photo courtesy of June Tailor, Inc.**

something new, the wrong pieces get seamed together and stitches need to be removed. I have seen students try to do this with shears because they haven't packed this seemingly obvious tool. Don't believe that mistakes won't happen to you. Be prepared for the worst case scenario. If the tool stays in your bag the whole class, great!

**Paper.** You probably go to a class to learn something new. You'll find that you get a lot more out of the class if you make notes. Even if handouts are provided, additional notes can be made to back up the information and make it clearer. The next time you read the instructions you were given in class, they should still make sense to you. In addition to regular lined paper, include some graph paper. The graph paper will make your drawings of grids or detailed instructions more proportionate and clearer.

**Binder.** Take a binder along to keep handouts and instruction sheets in. Often instruction sheets fall off the table onto the floor or inadvertently get left behind because they're loose and not packed in with other supplies. When they are immediately placed in a binder, instructions are still accessible, but are less likely to become lost or damaged. A hole punch is useful if handouts haven't been printed on 3-hole-punched paper.

**Pen and pencils.** Something to write with is essential for making notes. Pack a pen for notes as well as pencils for making diagrams. Take along an eraser or correction fluid to delete any incorrect notes so they won't confuse you later. I like to pack colored pencils for shading in different areas of a design. This makes the notes clearer to me. Many classrooms do not contain a pencil sharpener. In addition to writing tools, you may want to include one.

**Garbage bag.** I've been amazed at the number of classrooms that don't provide adequate garbage facilities. Take along a small lunch bag or plastic shopping bag and some tape. Tape the bag to the counter. It's much easier to work if you you're not constantly running back and forth to the garbage in an effort to keep the work surface clear.

**Luggage carrier.** End the juggling act of carrying the machine, your purse, a bag of supplies, and assorted extras by purchasing a luggage carrier. These are used in airports to help transport luggage from one airline to another. They fold down into small, flat packages and are easily stored. Even if you're only walking a few hundred feet, you'll find it's easier to load the machine and supplies onto this carrier and wheel it into class.

**Ironing surface.** In most classrooms, ironing surfaces are provided. However, if a great deal of pressing is required, or if there are many students, production will be slowed down by the amount of time spent waiting for an ironing surface. A portable ironing surface can be quite useful.

**Iron.** Of course, if you're taking an ironing surface to class, you'll also need to take an iron. Choose one that is lightweight, produces lots of steam, has a variety of temperature settings, and holds a large amount of water. A travel iron is easy to transport and can be quite useful in classroom situations, providing it produces sufficient steam. You'll need to refill it more often than a large iron, so include a water cup.

**Power bar.** A shortage of outlets can make juggling machine and pressing time frustrating. An electrical outlet bar has space for more than one tool at a time, with room to share space with other students.

## 2. TOOL CARRIERS

Besides all these wonderful tools, you need something to carry them around in. Rolykit, Inc., manufactures a wonderful sewing basket called the Rolyspace (Fig. 6–2). It isn't anything like the traditional basket we're used to. It's a compact 10″ × 9″ × 11″ that expands to a 35½″ width—like one of those kitchen cupboard organizers that keeps unfolding to expose more and more shelves. Sections are designed for thread spools, bobbins, scissors, buttons, needles, and other supplies. Everything is contained and visible. Just set it on the tabletop and keep right on being efficient and organized away from home. A carry handle makes it easy to transport. Omnigrid, Inc., manufactures a project bag for carrying rulers, mats, and materials. A variety of pockets are provided for the different squares and rulers as well as mats, fabric and paperwork. A clear pocket is provided for sharp tools to avoid accidentally cutting your hands. The handle and/or carrying strap makes it easy to carry around (Fig. 6–3). With these two organizational tools, you can contain and carry most classroom supplies.

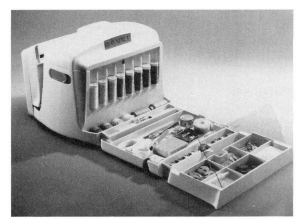 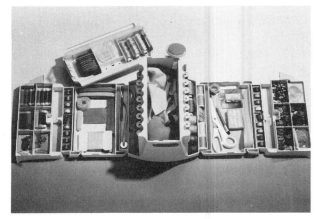

6–2. A storage box like the one pictured (a) closed and (b) open is useful for packing supplies. Photo courtesy of Rolykit, Inc.

6–3. A project bag is helpful for carrying flat materials like rulers and mats. Photo courtesy of Omnigrid, Inc.

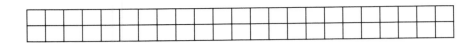

# · 7 ·

# Inside the Workroom: A List of Tools

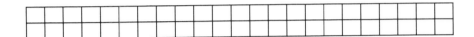

There are tools of all shapes and descriptions that simplify the sewing process. Tools like the dressmakers' hams and the seam rolls help press darts and seams to create a professional image. Smaller tools, like a collar point and tube turner or a bodkin, take the frustration out of turning small areas of fabric neatly and threading elastic and cording. Even a basic tool like beeswax is invaluable considering the amount of time you would waste untangling knotted threads if you didn't use it. The longer you sew, the more tools you'll collect.

Below is an alphabetical list of tools. You may have most of these or just a few. Some that were unknowns probably will become additions to your "wish list." Many sewing tool companies have catalogues of these and similar tools with pictures and descriptions. Write to them and ask for a copy of the latest catalogue, and see what is available. You'll probably find tools you didn't know existed. The correct tools improve the quality of your workmanship.

## 1. INVENTORY

I have included an inventory sheet (page 147). I can't stress enough how important it is to know—or at least have an idea of—the overall value of your sewing room and the tools you have there. Add the sewing machine and serger to this inventory as they don't appear in the following list but are expensive items in terms of replacement cost. Besides maintaining an inventory of tools, record your other equipment. Once the sewing studio has been established, very few additional furniture or equipment pieces will be purchased, so an inventory of these items is relatively easy to maintain.

My husband and I once made a small wager about who spent more money on "toys" in a year. Since his hobby of racing dirt bikes can be an expensive one, I figured I easily had spent less. I discovered at the end of our season that I had spent more than $3,000 on assorted fabric, notions, and patterns. It was more than I had anticipated, and an indication that the contents of my sewing room were worth a great deal of money. (And that was before I started sewing as much as I do now!)

If you're running a business, check with an accountant about the recordkeeping procedures you should follow. They may vary for different businesses, depending on the services provided, equipment, area of operation, depreciation of equipment, etc.

Even if you don't run a business, you should know the overall replacement cost of your sewing space. One way to do this is to record purchases on a calendar and keep a running total of the receipts for a year. Although this is definitely not an accurate, tax-acceptable method, it will give you an average value because you probably are using and purchasing similar supplies each year. Another method to determine the value is to do an inventory of existing supplies. Since these are constantly being replenished it too would be an average value.

## 2. TOOLS

**Beeswax.** Pulling a thread through this solid, resinous substance strengthens the thread, prevents knotting, and makes threading needles easier.

**Bias tape maker.** Cut bias fabric strips are fed into one end of this tape maker and are pressed with an iron into single-fold bias tape as they are pulled out the other end. Tape makers are available in ½", ¾", 1" and 2" widths.

**Bobbins.** Available in metal or plastic. The bobbin holds the lower thread in the sewing machine. Plastic bobbins are recommended for machines that use drop in bobbins, as they will not become magnetized.

**Bobbin box.** A small plastic box designed to hold bobbins, either wound or empty.

**Bobbin holders.** These clip onto the thread spool to hold bobbin and spool together. One manufacturer's bobbin holders are marketed under the name Handi-Bobs. They fit the spools of most brands.

**Bodkin.** A bodkin is an oversized needle with a blunt point and a safety-pin-like clasp at one end. It is used to thread ribbon, cording or elastic through a loop, hem, or casing.

**Button elevator.** Slipped between the button and the garment while the button is being stitched, this tool provides elevation, allowing you to form a shank after the button has been sewn by twisting thread around the stitches below the button.

**Chalk pencil.** Used to transfer markings on fabric. These pencils, available in several colors, allow fine chalk lines to be drawn on fabric, to indicate pattern markings.

**Chalk wheel.** A chalk wheel transfers markings from pattern to fabric accurately. They are available in blue and white. The chalk wheel is often preferred over a pencil, because there is no sharpening involved.

**Collar point and tube turner.** These are used for making spaghetti straps, buttonhole loops, and belts; the scissorlike tool instantly turns any point. It is also ideal for tailoring details, such as lapels, collar points, and pocket flaps.

**Cutting board.** A strong, portable cutting surface used during the layout and cutting steps of a project. Available in the standard size of 40" × 72" with one-inch grids for ease in laying fabric on grain. Many boards contain extra markings, such as lines for cutting bias strips, scallops, and circles. The cutting board folds up for easy storage.

**Dress form.** Available in various models. A dress form is a 3-dimensional model of your or your client's body proportions, making construction and fitting of garments easier.

**Dressmakers' carbon paper.** Traditionally used for fabric marking, carbon paper was used on the wrong side of fabrics, Now, papers are available that are air- and water-soluble, allowing marking on the right side of fabrics. Always pretest these products to ensure that no marks will remain on the fabric, however.

**Dressmakers' gauge.** Usually manufactured in clear plastic, this measuring device is marked off in inches (or cm) along one straight edge, while the other edge is scalloped; for marking short distances and making scallops or small curves.

**Dressmakers' ruler.** A combination of several measuring tools, this 4" × 15" clear plastic ruler is used for precision markings such as pleats and tucks. It is marked with metric and imperial measurements and parallel slots.

**Emery bag.** A small bag containing fine abrasive powder that is used to keep pins and needles sharp and rust free. Often, they are attached to a pin cushion and shaped like a strawberry.

**Glue basting liquid.** Applied in a thin liquid line, glue basting liquid works like a glue stick.

**Glue stick.** Can be used to adhere two fabrics together prior to stitching; for seams, underlining, trim, pockets, appliqués, etc.

**Hem gauge.** A metal measuring device used in conjunction with the iron to press up hems. One straight edge is marked off in inches for measuring straight hems; the other, gradually curved edge can be used for shaping rounded hems. Various different curve lines are marked for different hem widths.

**Hem marker.** Used to measure the skirt length and the hemline from the floor up. Three different types are available: pin, chalk, and a combination.

**Iron.** A necessity in the sewing room. The iron should be a steam–dry combination with an adjustable thermostat for use with all types of fabric.

**Ironing blanket.** Useful in situations where an ironing board is not available. It is a portable unit with a bonded, metallized cover making it heat-reflective, steam-permeable and scorch-resistant.

**Ironing board**. The ironing board is a firm pressing surface, adjustable in height, covered with a heat-resistant fabric. Tabletop, wall, and door-mounted models are available.

**Ironing board caddy**. Made up of two parts, a sturdy basket and a clip section which screws to the ironing board, the caddy is large enough to contain scissors, tape measure, marking pens, pins, etc. The basket lifts off for easy storage.

**Ironing board clothing rack.** This rack slips over the wide end of the ironing board, providing a convenient place to hang garments while pressing. One is marketed under the name Handy Hanger.

**Iron caddy**. The iron caddy clamps on to the end of the ironing board and holds the iron securely so that it cannot be displaced if the ironing board is jarred or bumped.

**Iron protector**. When placed over the sole plate of the iron, the special surface of the iron protector protects the iron from scorch marks or shine.

**Liquid seam sealant.** Liquid seam sealant is used to stop fabric fraying and prevent ravelling on ribbon edges or lace trim, also to finish raw fabric edges and stop runs in knit fabrics or nylons, or in areas of small detail.

**Loop turner.** A thin metal tool used to turn fabric tubing right-side out; used to make lingerie straps, loops, and belts.

**Marking pens for fabric.** Available in two versions: with water-soluble blue ink, designed for use on washable fabrics, and with evaporating purple ink. The purple ink marks disappear within 48 hours. These pens are used to transfer pattern markings such as pockets, pleats, or tucks from pattern pieces to fabric pieces. Always pretest these products on the fabrics you are planning to use.

**Needles.** Many different kinds are available for specialty uses: machine and hand-sewing, and for use on stretch fabrics, leather, denim, and double knits, for top stitching, etc.

**Needle board.** A firm surface, covered with short, blunt needles, that is used when pressing napped fabrics to prevent damage to the nap or the fabric surface.

**Needle case.** A small container, usually with a screw-on lid, used to store needles when they are not required.

**Needle grabber.** Used to grip a needle and pull it through heavy fabrics or leather with ease.

**Needle inserter.** Holds the needle firmly in place as the needle screw on a sewing machine is tightened.

**Needle threader.** Avoid the frustration of threading a needle by inserting this small wire tool through the eye of the needle and using it to pull the thread through.

**Notion rail.** A magnetic rail used to store metallized tools or notions.

**Pins.** Used to secure the pattern to the fabric prior to cutting out, or to hold garment pieces together for project construction. Dressmaker pins are preferred because they are thin, sharp, and therefore will not mar the fabric surface. Pins are also available with flat, round, plastic, or glass heads. When sewing with very fine fabric, purchase silk pins.

These are very fine, slender pins, designed not to damage the fabric. Ballpoint pins are recommended when sewing knits. The tiny ball-shaped point penetrates the fabric but does not catch or snag the fibres.

**Pin cushions.** Used to keep pins handy and ready for use. Available in the standard sawdust-filled form or in magnetic form. Magnetic pin-holders prevent pins from straying, are more inclined to catch the oddly thrown pin, and pick up spilled pins with ease. Wrist models are available in either the standard or magnetic versions. Magnetic pin-cushions will not work with nickel or brass pins.

**Pinking shears.** Used to finish raw edges on firmly woven fabrics that do not fray much.

**Pocket former template.** A metal plate with four different corners, used to shape the seam allowance on patch pockets to the appropriate curve.

**Point presser.** A platformlike tool with shaped extensions and points, designed to press small corner areas such as collars, facings, or cuffs.

**Point turner.** A small, flat tool with a slightly blunted tip, used to create neat, crisp points in areas such as collars, waistbands, or cuffs.

**Press cloth.** A firm cotton or cheesecloth used in the pressing process to prevent ridges, marred surfaces, or shiny spots from occurring on the fabric.

**Press mitt.** This overstuffed, rounded mitt is covered with wool fabric on one side and muslin on the other. Your hand fits inside to allow small, rounded areas to be pressed with ease.

**Pressing strips.** Paper strips are used under the seam allowance to prevent seam impressions from showing on the right side of the fabric after pressing.

**Puff iron.** A metal, egg-shaped dry-heat iron used to press puff sleeves or ruffles without danger of scorching delicate fabrics. Especially ideal for children's clothing or heirloom sewing projects.

**Push pins.** Large-headed pins used in conjunction with a cutting board to secure the pattern and fabric to the board, which may be pushed in with your thumb.

**Rotary cutter.** A hand-held tool, resembling a pizza cutter, that is used to cut fabric. The rotary cutter is extremely sharp and must be used with a rotary mat to protect the work surface.

**Rotary cutting mat.** A self-healing mat, available in several sizes, that protects your work surface from the sharp blade of the rotary cutter. Rotary cutting mats may be purchased with or without grids printed on their surfaces.

**Rotary ruler.** A 5″ to 6″ wide transparent ruler, gridded every ⅛″, used with the rotary cutting mat and the rotary cutter to cut straight edges and to cut quilt strips. Available in varying lengths.

**Ruler.** A 6″ plastic ruler is excellent for measuring short lengths, such as buttonholes, pockets or hems.

**Scissors and shears.** A good pair of stainless steel or nickel- or chrome-plated shears should be reserved for cutting fabric only. Treated properly, kept clean and sharp, a pair of scissors will last a lifetime. Quality scissors and shears are assembled with a screw and not a rivet.

Acquire a pair of shears 7" to 8" long, preferably with a bent handle, which prevents the fabric from lifting from the table during cutting. Sewing scissors approximately 5" long are used for clipping curves or trimming seams, and embroidery scissors 3" to 4" long are used for hand sewing. The difference between the terms *scissors* and *shears* lies in the size. Scissors range from approximately 3" to 6" in length; shears are 7" long or longer.

**Seam gauge.** A seam gauge is a 6" metal ruler with a sliding indicator, used to measure small distances such as hems, buttonholes, and pleats, or where quick, accurate measurements are necessary.

**Seam guide.** This tool is adhered to the machine bed magnetically or with a screw. Set the guide the desired distance from the needle, and run the fabric edge against it to ensure an even seam width.

**Seam ripper.** A seam ripper is used for removing incorrect stitches. It has one long and one short point, bridged by a very sharp curved edge between.

**Seam roll.** The seam roll is also called a sleeve roll. It is a long, firmly stuffed cushion that allows seams to be pressed open without indenting the fabric or making the seam visible from the right side of the fabric. One side of the seam roll is covered with wool fabric, the other with muslin.

**Simflex gauge.** This tool automatically divides an area into equal distances without the need for complicated calculating. It is useful for spacing pleats, tucks, shirring, buttons, or buttonholes.

**Sleeve board.** The sleeve board is similar in appearance to two small ironing boards attached together. The sleeve board is used to press narrow, hard-to-reach areas, darts, and curved seams.

**Stay tape.** Used to stabilize seams in areas such as shoulders, necklines, and curved seams, and to prevent stretching of the seam line, maintaining correct garment shaping.

**Styling curve.** Used for altering patterns, to redraw shaped or curved areas such as armholes, sleeve caps, necklines, and princess seams.

**Tailor's chalk.** Available in a range of colors, tailor's chalk can be made either of hard chalk or of soapstone. It is used for temporary markings such as hemlines or alterations. (Because a greasy stain may be left on the cloth, it is best to avoid wax-based chalk.)

**Tailor's ham.** The tailor's ham is firmly stuffed, with wool fabric on one side and muslin on the other. It is essential in pressing darts, seams, and sleeve caps.

**Tape measure.** A measuring tool used for all areas of project construction. Tape measures are made of linen, fibre glass, plastic, or treated paper with metal tips. Fiberglas and coated cloth tapes are considered the best choice, as they will not shrink or stretch. Pressure-sensitive tape measures are available to adhere to the sewing or cutting table.

**Thimble.** The thimble should fit snugly on the middle finger of your needle hand; it is used to help push the needles through the fabric as you stitch.

**Thread clippers.** A miniature pair of scissors used to snip threads. The handles are kept apart by a spring and are squeezed to move the blades.

| Description | Quantity | Price | Total |
|---|---|---|---|
| | | | |
| | | | |
| | | | |
| | | | |
| | | | |
| | | | |
| | | | |
| | | | |
| | | | |
| | | | |
| | | | |
| | | | |
| | | | |
| | | | |
| | | | |
| | | | |
| | | | |
| | | | |
| | | | |
| | | | |
| | | | |
| | | | |
| | | | |
| | | | |
| | | | |
| | | | |
| | | | |
| | | | |
| | | | |
| | | | |
| | | | |
| | | | |
| | | | |

7–1. Inventory form.

**Thread rack.** A rack used to organize standard-size thread spools or cone-size serger threads.

**Tracing wheel.** A tracing wheel is used in conjunction with carbon paper to transfer pattern markings. Tracing wheels are available in three types: sawtooth, for light to medium weight fabrics; needle-point, for heavier difficult to mark fabrics; and smooth-edge for fine, lightweight fabrics, suedes, leather, or vinyl, which would be permanently damaged from the small holes left by the other types of wheels.

**T Square.** A T-shaped ruler used to establish right angles, measure perpendicular lines, or to check the grain of fabric.

**Velvet board.** Similar to a needle board.

**Wash-away basting thread.** Used on washable fabric for areas of temporary stitching, prior to permanent stitching. Not suitable for dry-cleanable fabrics.

**Wash-away fabric adhesive.** Used on the back of pattern pieces to finger-press fabric in place for completely pinless "pinning." Excellent when working with fabrics such as leather or vinyl that can not be pinned, or for temporarily holding slippery fabrics such as silk or tricot. Will hold appliqués or trims in place while you do permanent stitching.

**Weights.** Small, flat weights can take the place of pins to hold pattern pieces in place while they are being cut out. Weights are often used in conjunction with the rotary cutting mat and cutter.

**Wooden clapper.** An oblong, wooden tool with two flat surfaces, used to flatten seams or hems without creating a hard, pressed look.

**Yardstick.** A 36″ to 40″ ruler used to draw marking lines on patterns, and to realign cutting lines on multisized patterns, or to measure hems.

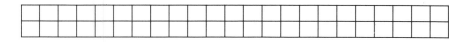

# · 8 ·

# Some Real-Life Sewing Spaces*

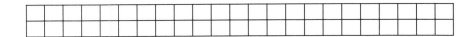

Did you ever read a decorating magazine and wonder where they get those perfect rooms? After all, real houses have limitations; they're not picture-perfect. For those of us living on an average budget, decorating can't run into tens of thousands of dollars, but this doesn't mean that we can't have cheerful and well-organized work spaces.

The sewing rooms represented here belong to real people. I didn't photograph any staged showrooms. These rooms come with the same limitations that you may find present in your own home. Let's look at how each seamstress solved her sewing space problems; the solutions may help you in setting up your sewing space.

## A SMALL SEWING ROOM

The space shown in the photo of Becky Drinkwater's room (Fig. 8–1) is virtually the total area. There is barely enough room left to set up an ironing board. A beautiful window looks into the sewing room from the kitchen, adding more light and depth. The light-colored walls and cupboards add to the sense of space. Patterned carpet and curtains create color and texture.

*Cutting:* To the right of the picture, there is a long counter that is sufficient for cutting out most garments or crafts projects. The width of the counter accommodates 45″ fabrics, folded. Rotary equipment or scissors can be used in this area.

*Construction:* Becky has placed her sewing machine and serger on the counter beside each other; she can thus slide from one to the other.

*Pressing:* Because the room is so narrow, Becky can swivel her chair around to press materials on the ironing board behind her. By lowering the position of the board, she can remain seated while pressing. Pressed garments are hung on a special rack designed for that purpose, which attaches to the ironing board.

*Note: Full-color photos of the rooms discussed in this chapter are shown in the color insert.

**8–1. Becky Drinkwater's small sewing room has a view of the yard and hills beyond.**

*Fitting:* This is the one area of the room that is lacking. However, since Becky is sewing for enjoyment, it's also the area that is the least critical. There's no room for a mirror or fitting area. Fitting must be done in another room.

*Storage:* For the size of this room there is plenty of storage space available: overhead cupboards and drawers. There's also under-counter or above-counter space available, if needed.

*Summary:* Even with its size limitations, this room meets the majority of Becky's requirements. With its placement, just off the kitchen and living areas, Becky can keep track of meals and family while still enjoying the privacy of her own space and the serenity of a beautiful view.

## A BASEMENT CRAFTS WORKROOM

Barb Howell's space (Fig. 8–2) is at one end of a narrow basement laundry room. The room is actually pink, but the natural sunlight from two windows, combined with incandescent lighting, highlights a warm, cosy, and inviting color scheme.

*Cutting:* The raised countertop is the perfect surface for cutting out, as well as assembling, projects, without bending or back strain. Its extra depth accommodates all widths of fabric, as well as large rotary cutting mats.

*Construction:* Probably the biggest limitation of the room is its

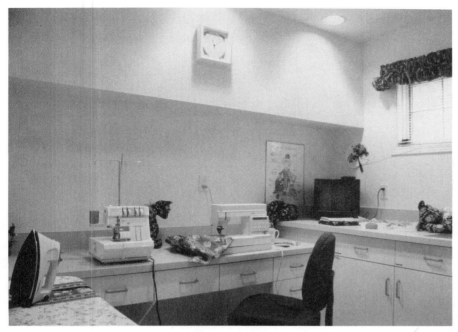

**8–2. Barb Howell's basement crafts room.**

construction area. Like Becky, Barb has placed her sewing machine and serger beside each other on the counter. Considering the width of the room and her needs, this is probably the best solution. The only other one she could consider would be to have an additional counter built where the ironing board is, making the construction area more L-shaped, and doing her pressing on a pressing mat on the raised countertop instead.

*Pressing:* The ironing board is placed at right angles to the construction surface, forming one side of a U-shaped work center in which it is easy to move around and work. The height of the ironing board can be adjusted if necessary.

*Fitting:* Because the room is long and narrow, Barb could mount a mirror on the wall opposite the sewing machines and use the room for fitting purposes if she wanted to.

*Storage:* With the different crafts Barb produces, many supplies require storage; some are quite bulky. There is storage space below the raised counter top for fabric, stuffing, fun furs, laces, trims, and decorations. Drawers at the cutting and construction surfaces hold tools and equipment.

*Summary:* Although in the basement, this space is wonderfully bright and airy. There is plenty of space in which to move around and work. Barb has the added bonus of a washer, dryer, and sink in the room. Located off the family room, she has easy access to the rest of the family.

8–3. Mary Scott's cottage industry produces children's clothes.

## A COTTAGE INDUSTRY PRODUCING CHILDREN'S CLOTHES

Out of this room (Fig. 8–3), Mary Scott operates Spectrum Fabricworks Ltd., "rainboWear for Kids," a highly productive cottage industry manufacturing about 15,000 articles of children's clothing per year. Two employees use the cutting area to cut out clothing, which is bundled, along with trim and thread, for completion by 13 seamstresses who work out of their own homes and sewing rooms. Working daily in this room are the cutters, one secretary, and the designer, Mary. There is additional work space not shown in this photo, where shelves of completed orders wait for sales personnel to deliver them, and where precut packages are stored for seamstresses to pick up and complete. The room, lit with fluorescent lighting, is bright.

*Cutting:* Garments are cut out using the central cutting surface from the fabrics lined up on the shelves behind the table and beneath it. Numbered boxes contain matching ribbing and trims. Paper patterns are clipped and hung numerically on the corner rack. Rotary equipment is used to speed-cut the patterns. An order book lists the various styles, sizes, and colors to be cut.

*Construction:* A U-shaped construction area is Mary's; here, she designs and sews prototypes and makes minor adjustments to completed garments.

*Pressing:* With an ironing board behind her sewing center,

8–4. Jeanne Chambers makes craft items and stuffed animals in this home sewing room.

Mary simply turns her chair and presses while she works. A department-store style clothing rack holds finished garments.

*Storage:* Mary's business has been growing by leaps and bounds, so her need for supplies also has increased. Another room in the house now stores excess fabrics and supplies. The ones currently used are kept on shelves in well-marked boxes.

*Fitting:* Before beginning construction, Mary measured a variety of children in each age range to determine average measurements, and designed her garments accordingly. Orders are placed based on the child's age or size.

*Summary:* This studio was designed for maximum productivity for its space. Plenty of room was left for employees to move about. A coffee center and stereo system provide additional comforts.

## A CRAFTS SEWING ROOM

Jeanne Chambers runs Colonial Crafts (Fig. 8–4); she produces a wide variety of craft items, ranging from stuffed animals to fabric boxes, for resale at craft shows and in various shops.

*Cutting:* There are two cutting areas. The first, to the left of the sewing center, doubles as an assembly surface. Large sheets of pegboard on the walls hold tools and hoops. Another cutting surface is used primarily for cutting fabrics. Fabrics stored on the shelves behind can be cut with rotary equipment arranged on the

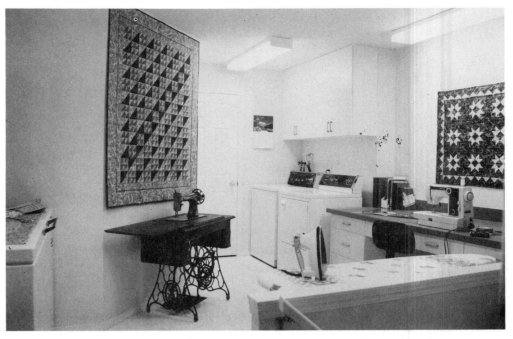

**8–5. Ruth Goertzen has a large personal sewing center in her laundry room.**

surface and then returned to the shelves immediately, eliminating any clutter.

*Construction:* Many of Jeanne's projects don't require much sewing. With the ready-made sewing center, she has sufficient work space without taking up more floor space. The sewing machine and serger are beside each other.

*Pressing:* Jeanne has an ironing board and tabletop pressing surfaces. For small jobs, the tabletop model is easier to reach and more accessible. Both are located by the cutting/assembly surface. Pressing supplies are stored on a shelf nearby.

*Storage:* Shelves at the right of the room contain well-labeled see-through plastic boxes with notions, trims, "body parts," and accessories. A large dresser contains odds and ends and patterns. Under the cutting surface is an assortment of wicker baskets.

*Summary:* I found this room seemed to draw me in. It was so warm and inviting. The antiques that decorate it were irresistible and the crafted creatures, enticing.

## A LARGE PERSONAL SEWING SPACE

Ruth Goertzen's sewing space (Fig. 8–5) is part of her laundry room. As traffic from the garage and the basement flows through the room, she needs to leave accessible floor space, which can't be tied up with cutting tables and various furniture pieces. Ruth sews in spurts and only for personal pleasure, so the arrangement she has works for her.

*Cutting:* Since the freezer is in the room, its large top naturally became the cutting surface. Ruth could easily use a large cutting mat on it. The counter with the sewing machine extends to the right over the stairwell, and is more difficult to reach; however, it provides extra space for longer lengths of fabric.

*Construction:* The wide counter-top area is an excellent construction space. Ruth at present has only a traditional sewing machine, but is contemplating a serger, which could go on another set of cabinets where the ironing board is currently. However, there is plenty of counter length and leg room for the machines to sit side by side. When she is not sewing, Ruth removes her machine from the counter and stores it, leaving the counter available for folding laundry or other projects.

*Pressing:* The ironing board, whose height is adjustable, is at right angles to the construction surface. Pressed clothes are hung in the closet by the back door.

*Fitting:* As the room has little privacy, it's not ideal for fitting garments. Other rooms in the house serve this purpose.

*Storage:* Cupboards above the freezer, washer, and dryer are used for storing sewing and laundry supplies. Drawers at the construction surface hold sewing and pressing tools, fabrics, and patterns.

*Summary:* Ruth's room is functional, practical, and spacious, and centrally located in the house.


## A QUILTER'S SEWING ROOM PLUS OFFICE

Remember that wish list I gave you in the beginning of the book? Well, when I tried to fit everything into the space that I had, it simply wasn't going to work. The biggest drawback was that, being in the basement, I couldn't see the backyard. With three children, it was important that they could go out and play while I worked. So after I looked around our house and discovered that the master bedroom was perfect for what I wanted, we simply rearranged things. Our new bedroom has a view of the valley and a fireplace. Very romantic! My sewing room has virtually everything I wanted (Fig. 8–6).

*Cutting:* This is probably the one drawback of the room. I use the desk surfaces for cutting out simple projects, but they are a bit too low. I'm not very tall myself, so it works for the most part, but if I'm going to be working on a project with continuous cutting, such as a quilt, I raise the level of one desk with blocks or set up my portable table. Either one works well, it just depends on how long I'll need the surface. For very long projects, I raise the desk; for the shorter ones, I use the portable table.

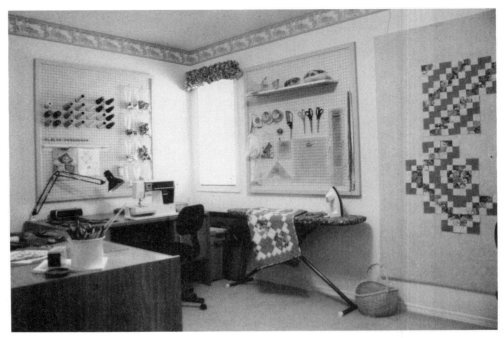

**8–6. This workroom plus office was formerly the master bedroom in the author's home.**

*Construction:* The desks provide a 30″ × 50″ construction surface. The drawers and cupboards hold extra supplies. I've placed them in an L-shape so the sewing machine can be placed on one and the serger on the other, making it a simple matter to turn back and forth. Because I do a lot more quilting than garment sewing, I remove the serger to a storage shelf nearby when it's not in use. Though I really like the look of custom-made cabinets, I chose not to use them here. When we move, the next owner may not be as appreciative of a sewing room in the master bedroom as I am!

*Pressing:* Usually I'll prefer to press fabrics standing up. It's simpler to lower the ironing board and swivel back and forth, but I sew for quite long periods of time and find it a nice break to stand up every once in a while. When I'm short on time, I lower the board and remain seated. I have a variety of pressing surfaces, from the standard ironing surface to tabletop models and pressing mats.

*Fitting:* One of the nice benefits of stealing the master bedroom is that there's a bathroom attached to my sewing room. It provides a convenient place for fitting garments. For quilt fittings, I have a large flannel board on the wall between the construction surfaces and my desk.

*Storage:* Each of the desk units provides storage with three drawers and a cupboard. In addition to that there's a set of shelves to the left of the room for magazines, pattern catalogues, my stereo, and the serger. I have some fabrics on the shelves also, which provide color and inspiration. To the right of my desk is a 6' closet, where I can keep my boxes of sewing and quilting supplies. Two large pegboards, one above the construction surface and the other above the ironing board, hold thread supplies, bobbins, rotary cutters and rulers, pressing tools, and various other supplies.

*Summary:* Besides the sewing requirements, my room also had to meet my business needs. The desk, computer, phone, and filing system take up one corner of the room. It's easy enough to work back and forth from the actual sewing to the computer when putting together designs. On the desk in the lower picture, you'll see some paper and colored pencils. I've placed some stools in front of this surface for my children to color with me, or for guests/clients to use when in my office. When friends come to sew, they set up their machines in this spot. With two bright windows, a view of the backyard and mountains, cheerful colors, and lots of space, my office is a dream to work in.

# About the Author

Myrna Giesbrecht lives in Kamloops, British Columbia, Canada, with her husband, daughter and two sons. She started out her work life intending to be a teacher and along the way has been a dispatcher, accounts payable clerk, hairstylist, fabric sales clerk, interior designer, quilting instructor and receptionist—all jobs from which she's been able to gather experience for operating her own company, in which she works as an author and quilt artist.

For Myrna, it's been a natural progression from taking classes and reading books to teaching seminars and putting together manuscripts. *Setting Up Your Sewing Space: From Small Areas to Complete Workshops* is a combination of Myrna's natural skills for organization and the techniques she has developed to make sewing not only functional and efficient but, more importantly, enjoyable and creative.

# A Word of Thanks

I would like to thank all the suppliers who so freely produced pictures of their products for inclusion in this text and who appeared as enthused and eager for this book as I am. It wouldn't be nearly as complete without their help: American Homeware; Butterick Company, Inc.; Clotilde, Inc.; Cottage Mills Inc.; EZ International; Horn of America; Fellowes Manufacturing; Fiskars, Inc.; Ideal Creations; June Tailor, Inc.; Little Foot, Ltd.; Me Sew Inc.; Mildred's Winning Combinations; Nancy's Notions; Omnigrid, Inc.; Polder, Inc.; Rolykit, Inc.; Salem Mfg. Co., Inc.; Sew/Fit Company; Tacony Corporation; Ultimate Marking Pencil; Voster Marketing; and Wood-Tec.

# Index

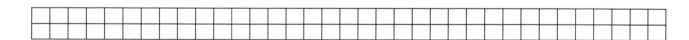